The Lincoln Way

GREAT
Presidential
DECISIONS

The *L*incoln Way

JEFFREY MORRIS

LERNER PUBLICATIONS COMPANY
MINNEAPOLIS

To Deborah,
who cannot help but make people love her

Previous page: After four years of civil war, Abraham Lincoln rode in triumph into the Confederate capital at Richmond, Virginia. His decision to fight to preserve the Union was one of the most significant ever made by a United States president.

Copyright © 1996 by Jeffrey B. Morris
Published by arrangement with Lou Reda Productions, Inc.

Library of Congress Cataloging-in-Publication Data

Morris, Jeffrey Brandon, 1941-
    The Lincoln way / by Jeffrey B. Morris.
        p. cm. — (Great presidential decisions)
    Includes index.
    ISBN 0-8225-2930-0
    1. Lincoln, Abraham, 1809–1865—Juvenile literature.
2. United States—Politics and government—Civil War, 1861–1865—Decision making—Juvenile literature. 3. Decision making—United States—History—19th century—Juvenile literature. [1. Lincoln, Abraham, 1809–1865. 2. Presidents. 3. United States—Politics and government—Civil War, 1861-1865. 4. Decision making.] I. Title. II. Series.
E457.905.MG7 1996
973.7'092—dc20   94-23754
                                                            CIP
                                                             AC

Manufactured in the United States of America

1 2 3 4 5 6 – JR – 01 00 99 98 97 96

Contents

Introduction

*T*HE AMERICANS WHO WROTE THE Constitution of the United States faced an unusual opportunity. They wanted to give American presidents enough power to make important decisions but not enough power to become a monarch. They wanted to protect the rights of citizens by limiting the power of the president.

Their country had won independence from Great Britain, which had a monarchical government. Most European nations at that time were governed by monarchies—by kings and queens. But Americans wanted a republic, a form of government in which power resides with those citizens who are entitled to vote. The government is run by elected officers and representatives who are responsible to the citizenry and who govern according to law.

The framers of the United States Constitution wanted a government powerful enough to protect

George Washington presided over the Constitutional Convention in Philadelphia in 1787, where he and his fellow delegates wrote the United States Constitution.

We the People

The Constitution begins "We the people," showing that the American government is elected by the people and is responsible to them.

the country from foreign enemies, but not powerful enough to take away the rights of the citizens. To accomplish this goal, they created a complex form of government. The framers divided the powers of the new government among three branches. They thought that the least powerful branch would be the judiciary. That branch was supposed to hear and decide lawsuits, decide disputes between the U.S. government and individual states, and keep the other two branches within their constitutional powers.

The framers expected the legislative branch, the Senate and the House of Representatives, to be the most powerful. Congress was supposed to make laws, levy taxes, and choose how to spend money.

The framers of the Constitution had the most trouble agreeing on the powers of the executive

branch. The head of that branch is the president. The framers wanted a president who could act speedily and forcefully. On the other hand, they definitely did not want someone with the powers of a king or dictator. The president would be elected for four years. He or she would be commander in chief of the military forces, would be primarily responsible for relations with other countries, and would ensure that the laws passed by Congress would be carried out. The president could also veto laws passed by Congress, but Congress could override that veto.

The framers thought that each branch of government would work at a different rate of speed, because each would each have its own set of duties. They thought the judicial branch would act most slowly, partly because lawyers usually need time to gather evidence and present their case, and because fair decisions require careful deliberation. The framers of the Constitution thought Congress would also act relatively slowly, because of the need to gather information, debate the issues, and get agreement among

Pictured, *left to right,* are Alexander Hamilton, James Madison, Charles Cotesworth Pinckney, Benjamin Franklin, Roger Sherman, and Elbridge Gerry. All were framers of the U.S. Constitution.

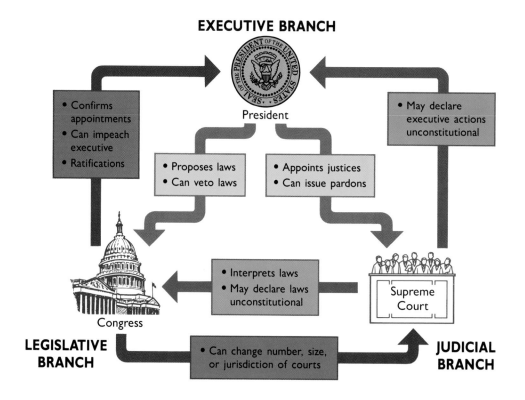

EXECUTIVE BRANCH

President

- Confirms appointments
- Can impeach executive
- Ratifications

- May declare executive actions unconstitutional

- Proposes laws
- Can veto laws

- Appoints justices
- Can issue pardons

Congress

- Interprets laws
- May declare laws unconstitutional

Supreme Court

LEGISLATIVE BRANCH

- Can change number, size, or jurisdiction of courts

JUDICIAL BRANCH

many members. The framers, however, wanted the president to be able to act rapidly and decisively.

When they drafted the Constitution, the framers expected that the Supreme Court would only meet at the nation's capital for a few months each year. But they intended that the president, even if he was away from the capital, would act for the nation in an emergency. The framers also wanted to be sure that in some areas—such as dealing with other nations—the United States should be as unified as possible, and they hoped that the president would express that unity. For these reasons—speed, unity, and the ability to act in an emergency—the framers expected that the president would often be called upon to make important decisions.

This book is one in a series about the great decisions that some of our presidents have made.

Of course, presidents make decisions every day. They decide whom to appoint to office, what to say to leaders of foreign nations, whether or not to veto laws passed by Congress. Most of these decisions are quite ordinary. From time to time, however, the president makes a decision that will affect the American people (and often other nations as well) for many years, maybe even centuries. You may think of Franklin Roosevelt's decision to fight the Great Depression, or John Kennedy's decision to fight for civil rights for African Americans. Of course, not every important decision our presidents have made has been wise. James Buchanan decided not to stop the Southern states from leaving the Union. Franklin Roosevelt decided to ask Congress to increase the size of the Supreme Court, so it would more often decide cases the way he wanted. Richard Nixon decided to cover up the Watergate burglary.

This book is about the decisions made by Abraham Lincoln, who may have been our greatest president. Serving in America's most troubled time, the Civil War, Lincoln made two of the most important decisions a president has ever made—to preserve the Union and to free the slaves. Lincoln also made countless other important decisions. Two of these were his choice of generals and his decision not to give into congressional pressure to change his cabinet. Besides showing how Lincoln went about making decisions, the following chapters also reveal what an unusual and remarkable man Abraham Lincoln was.

Both of these symbols, the American flag and the Great Seal, reflect American values. In the Great Seal, the eagle holds an olive branch and arrows, reminding us that the United States desires peace, but will wage war if necessary.

America in 1861

ON MARCH 4, 1861, ABRAHAM LINcoln became president of the fastest growing nation in the world. The population of the United States had grown to a little over 31 million—eight times greater than when George Washington had been president 70 years before. The people of the United States had the highest standard of living in the world. American industry produced more goods than any country in the world except Great Britain.

In a little more than 15 years, vast areas in the West had been added to the United States. Texas, which was then an independent nation, joined the United States. The United States won a huge area (the present states of California, Nevada, Utah, and

The United States was a fast-growing nation in 1861. Railroads helped unite the country as it expanded westward, but other forces were pulling it apart.

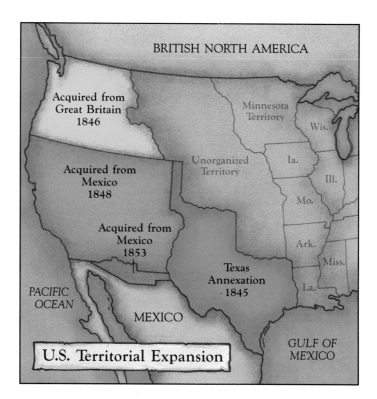

U.S. Territorial Expansion

The nation pushed westward to the Pacific Ocean in the mid-1800s. Between 1845 and 1861, when Lincoln became president, the area of the United States increased by 60 percent. One huge tract of land in the Pacific Northwest was ceded to the United States by Great Britain. The rest came from Mexico.

most of Arizona) in a war with Mexico. A treaty with Great Britain added most of what is now the Pacific Northwest. Still more land (what became the southern part of Arizona and New Mexico) was acquired by another treaty with Mexico.

Explorers, traders, and others had told of rich soil and abundant game in much of the western lands. By the 1840s, many Americans began moving west to farm and ranch and mine for gold. Communities of pioneers sprang up everywhere. As an area became more settled, it could become a territory. Later, a territory could become a state.

The continent was also being united by railroad. In fact, the United States had a larger network of railroads than the rest of the world combined. During the early part of the century, it had taken 52 days to ship crops by boat and wagon from the middle of the country in Cincinnati, Ohio, to New York City in the East. But by 1861, crops took only 5 days to travel the same distance by railroad. Where railroads did not yet run, roads were being built.

Communication in 1861 had also greatly improved. About a year before Lincoln was elected, riders of the Pony Express began carrying mail on horseback from Missouri to California. The riders could travel that route in just 10 days. Even better, about six months after Lincoln's election, the transcontinental telegraph opened. News that had taken weeks to travel a few hundred miles when Washington became president now took just hours to cross the country by telegraph.

But railroads and roads and telegraph lines were not enough to unite a nation. The United States was not united. In fact, by 1861, it was breaking apart.

Half Slave, Half Free

The most important reason that the United States was splitting apart was slavery. About half the states in 1861 allowed slavery (mostly those in the South). The other half (mostly in the North) didn't. Neither side wanted the other to get larger.

Congress passed laws trying to keep both Southerners and Northerners happy by keeping the number of slave states and free states equal. One law, passed in 1820, was the Missouri Compromise. It drew a line across the United States at a latitude of 36° 30'. States above the line would all be free; those below the line would allow slavery.

PUTTING UP TELEGRAPH WIRES

The transcontinental telegraph was completed shortly after Lincoln became president.

But what about slavery in America's new lands? If slavery was allowed in a territory, that might eventually lead to a new slave state. If slavery was forbidden there, a new free state would be added. The balance between free and slave states might be lost.

Besides, by the 1840s, abolitionists (those who opposed slavery) were no longer concerned just about keeping a balance. They didn't see how they could ban slavery in the slave states, but they did want to keep slavery from spreading westward. They took the battle to Congress, where Southern congressmen opposed them.

Finally, in 1850, a compromise was worked out. It said, in part, that settlers in the territories of New Mexico and Utah (which were then much larger than the present states with those names) could decide the issue of slavery for themselves. Other territories would still follow the line of the Missouri Compromise.

Many hoped this solution, called the Compromise of 1850, would settle the problem of slavery in the territories. But it didn't work for long. Several years later, a man who was probably the most influential member of Congress at that time reopened the debate. Senator Stephen Douglas of Illinois proposed changing the rules for two territories, Kansas and Nebraska. Under the Missouri Compromise and the Compromise of 1850, Nebraska should be free, and Kansas slave. Instead, Douglas argued, the settlers in both should decide for themselves, just as the people of New Mexico and Utah could.

Senator Stephen Douglas believed settlers should decide for themselves whether to allow slavery. A small man, he was called "The Little Giant."

Congress agreed. Douglas was able to get what we know as the Kansas-Nebraska Act passed in 1854. But his proposal caused much bitterness. Many citizens, including Abraham Lincoln, saw the act as

Plantation owners in the South in the 1800s thought that slave labor was essential for a healthy Southern economy. If the balance of power tipped to the free states, they feared slavery would be outlawed and they would face financial ruin.

an attempt to perpetuate slavery. They thought slavery would die out gradually in the slave states if it was not allowed to spread to the territories. Some citizens organized a new political party, the Republican Party, that year to oppose slavery in all the territories.

Over the next six years, the situation worsened. Fighting broke out in Kansas between those who wanted it slave and those who wanted it free. About 200 people were killed, and two million dollars in property was destroyed. In the wake of this violence, Kansas became known as "Bleeding Kansas."

That same year, a leading abolitionist senator,

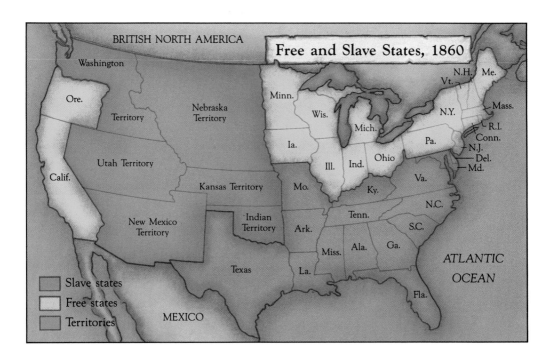

Free and Slave States, 1860

BRITISH NORTH AMERICA

Washington

Ore.

Nebraska
Territory

Minn.

Wis.

Mich.

N.H. Me.
Vt.

N.Y.

Mass.

R.I.
Conn.
Pa.
N.J.
Del.
Md.

Utah Territory

Calif.

Ia.

Ill. Ind. Ohio

Va.

Kansas Territory

Mo.

Ky.

New Mexico
Territory

Indian
Territory

Ark.

Tenn.

N.C.

S.C.

Texas

La.

Miss. Ala. Ga.

ATLANTIC
OCEAN

Fla.

Slave states

Free states

Territories

MEXICO

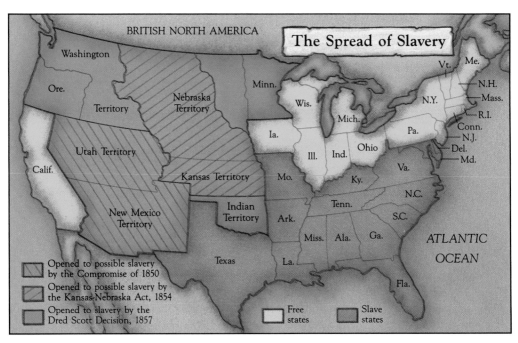

The Spread of Slavery

BRITISH NORTH AMERICA

Washington

Ore.

Nebraska
Territory

Minn.

Wis.

Mich.

Vt. Me.

N.H.

N.Y.

Mass.

R.I.
Conn.
Pa.
N.J.
Del.
Md.

Utah Territory

Calif.

Ia.

Ill. Ind. Ohio

Va.

Kansas Territory

Mo.

Ky.

New Mexico
Territory

Indian
Territory

Ark.

Tenn.

N.C.

S.C.

Texas

La.

Miss. Ala. Ga.

ATLANTIC
OCEAN

Fla.

Opened to possible slavery
by the Compromise of 1850

Opened to possible slavery by
the Kansas-Nebraska Act, 1854

Opened to slavery by the
Dred Scott Decision, 1857

Free
states

Slave
states

Charles Sumner of Massachusetts, gave a speech entitled "The Crime Against Kansas." Enraged by Sumner's speech, a Southern member of the U.S. House of Representatives attacked Sumner with a cane so violently that Sumner almost died. Many Northerners were horrified. In the South, many cheered the attacker.

But perhaps more than any other event, a Supreme Court ruling in 1857 helped push the North and South apart. In the Dred Scott case, the Court decided that Congress had no power to draw a line banning slavery in some territories. The U.S. Constitution, they said, allowed slavery. For that reason, the compromises of the past were not constitutional.

By now, feelings about slavery were heated. Some furious Northerners, including Lincoln, argued that the Supreme Court decision was not fair. They thought some politicians, including Stephen Douglas and President James Buchanan, had conspired with Chief Justice Roger B. Taney and had influenced the ruling. What would come next? Maybe the Supreme Court would decide slavery must be allowed everywhere.

Opposite, before the Civil War, the United States was split into free states, slave states, and territories. Several laws in the 1800s allowed slavery to spread westward.

By 1858, Abraham Lincoln thought the United States would have to be all one thing or all another. Running for the United States Senate, he told voters, "A house divided against itself cannot stand. I believe this government cannot endure half slave and half free."

The following year a white abolitionist decided to take matters into his own hands. John Brown led a raid on the United States arsenal at Harpers Ferry, Virginia. He hoped to start a revolt of slaves by seizing the arsenal and distributing the weapons. But the effort was a feeble one—Brown took just 18 men with him. And no slaves joined him. The revolt failed, and Brown was executed.

Still, the South was horrified. What if Brown had succeeded and masses of slaves had revolted? The South celebrated Brown's death, while the North mourned it.

The violence in Kansas, the attack on Charles

The Dred Scott Case

*D*red Scott was a slave who moved with his master from a slave state to a free state and then back. They lived first in Missouri (a slave state), moved to Illinois and then to Wisconsin Territory (which both banned slavery), and then returned to Missouri. Scott didn't think his master could legally keep him as a slave, since they had lived in areas where slavery was banned. In 1846, Scott sued for his freedom.

The Supreme Court heard the case, known as *Scott v. Sanford.* In 1857, it decided against Scott by a vote of 7-2. Scott had sued from Missouri, so Missouri's laws applied, the Court ruled. Since Missouri allowed slavery, Scott was a slave.

Besides, the Court said, Scott shouldn't have been able to sue in the first place. It held that African Americans could never be citizens of the United States, and only citizens have the right to be heard in court.

Additionally, the Court held that Congress did not have the power under the Constitution to prohibit or abolish slavery in the territories. By denying Congress that power over slavery, the Court made a political compromise over slavery almost impossible.

Many Northerners revered John Brown and mourned when he was led to his execution, but Southerners feared him. The two views of Brown, *above*, reflect the growing division between them.

Sumner, the outrage over the Dred Scott decision, and the raid by John Brown showed that Lincoln was right. The United States could not endure half slave and half free. For the slave states, the election of Abraham Lincoln as president in 1860 was the last straw.

Starting Out

THE STORY OF ABRAHAM LIN-
coln's life may already be known to you.
He was born in a log cabin on February
12, 1809, in Hodgenville, Kentucky (about 45 miles
south of the Indiana border, near Louisville). His
father, Thomas Lincoln, owned a 300-acre farm
there. When Abraham was two years old, he and
his parents and his older sister, Sarah, moved 8 miles
away to Knob Creek, an area of rocky cliffs, tall trees,
and clear streams.

Five years later the family moved again. This time
they went to Indiana, settling in what Lincoln
remembered as "an unbroken forest," "a wild region
with many bears and other wild animals." During
their first winter there, the family survived on wild
game, birds, honey, nuts, and wild fruit. By the time

Young Abraham probably didn't spend more than a year in school
when he was growing up. But he educated himself, reading as
many books as he could find.

This cabin is a replica of one believed to be Abraham's birthplace in Kentucky.

he was eight, Abraham had already been put to work with an ax, clearing the land.

Abraham's mother, Nancy Hanks Lincoln, died when he was nine. A year later his father remarried. His new wife was Sarah Johnston, a widow with three children. In Abraham's words, she "proved a good and kind mother."

Abraham had little formal schooling, probably no more than a year. But he was a great reader, walking miles to borrow books. He explained his education this way:

> Of course when I came of age I did not know much. Still somehow, I could read, write, and cipher to the Rule of Three; but that was all. The little advance I now have upon this store of education, I have picked up from time to time under the pressure of necessity.

Abraham spent his teenage years in Indiana. When he was 19, he got a job taking a load of crops to New Orleans. Abraham and another man built a flatboat and guided it through 1,200 miles of the Ohio and Mississippi rivers. The year Abraham turned 21, his family moved to southern Illinois. He stayed with them long enough to help split fence rails, build a cabin, and plant corn, before finally striking out on his own.

Lincoln settled in the village of New Salem, Illinois, 20 miles northwest of Springfield. There he spent six years working at many jobs. He managed a mill and ran a store. He also served as village postmaster and did some surveying. It was in New Salem that Lincoln studied law and entered politics. He rose rapidly in politics. He was elected to the state legislature at the age of 25 and was reelected three times. By the age of 28, he had become the leader of an important political party, the Whig Party, in the Illinois House of Representatives.

Lincoln was still quite poor, however. In fact, when he moved to Springfield in 1837, he rode on a borrowed horse and carried all his possessions in two saddlebags. In Springfield he met and married Mary Todd, who belonged to a prominent Kentucky family. Their first son, Robert, was born in 1843. Three more boys followed—Edward in 1846, Willy in 1850, and Tad in 1853.

Lincoln served just one term in the United States House of Representatives (from 1847 to 1849). There he urged the abolition of slavery in the District of Columbia. He opposed the Mexican War (which he said was "unnecessarily begun" by then President James K. Polk). But the United States did fight the

Mary Todd came from a prominent Kentucky family. She was visiting relatives in Illinois when she met Abraham Lincoln.

Until 1855, Lincoln was a leader of the Whig Party in Illinois. He joined the Republican Party in that year.

war and acquired new territory when it won. Lincoln voted to ban slavery in the new land.

Lincoln's antiwar views made him unpopular back in Illinois. His political career came to a standstill, if not an end, and Lincoln turned to the practice of law. Here, too, he rose rapidly. While he represented many "little people," he also represented rich and powerful companies such as the McCormick Reaper Company and the Illinois Central Railroad. He argued some 243 cases before the Illinois Supreme Court—a very large number—and won most of them. In those days, judges and lawyers held court all over the state, traveling and rooming together. Lincoln may well have been at his happiest during these days, swapping stories with lawyers, judges, and country folk.

Lincoln stayed out of politics from 1849 to 1854. The controversy over slavery in Kansas and Nebraska deeply gripped him, however, and he returned to politics. Lincoln was opposed to the Kansas-Nebraska Act. He feared the act would make it impossible to end slavery. Like many others, Lincoln believed that if slavery could be prevented from spreading, it would die out. In 1855, a year after the Republican Party was created to oppose slavery in the territories, Lincoln joined it.

Over the next few years, the Republican Party gained in strength in the North. The events in "Bleeding Kansas," the Dred Scott decision, and the fate of John Brown attracted many supporters. Many Democrats and Whigs who were antislavery joined.

The Whig Party

*T*he Whig Party began in the 1830s as a party opposed to Andrew Jackson and his Democratic Party. Many, but not all, Whigs supported assistance by the United States government for the building of roads and canals, the creation of a national bank, and a high tariff. The greatest leaders of the Whig Party were Senators Daniel Webster of Massachusetts and Henry Clay of Kentucky. Two presidents, William Henry Harrison (1840) and Zachary Taylor (1848), were also Whigs. In the 1850s the party split into Northern and Southern wings, then collapsed. Many of the Northern Whigs joined the Republican Party when it was created in 1854.

Lincoln spoke out against the spread of slavery during the Lincoln-Douglas debates of 1858.

Meanwhile, Lincoln became one of the top leaders of the party in Illinois.

As the party grew, Lincoln soon began to be nationally known as well. In 1856 he almost got the Republican nomination for vice president. He received 110 votes at the Republican convention. That wasn't enough to gain him the nomination—but at least Republicans were beginning to know who he was.

In 1858 Lincoln did win a Republican nomination—to run for the United States Senate. His opponent was the man who had proposed the

Kansas-Nebraska Act, Senator Stephen Douglas. Accepting the nomination, Lincoln uttered words that would be heard throughout the nation:

> A house divided against itself cannot stand. I believe this government cannot endure permanently, half slave and half free. I do not expect the Union to be dissolved—I do not expect the house to fall—but I do expect it will cease to be divided. It will become all one thing or all the other.

Lincoln and Douglas joined in seven debates, beginning in August and ending in October. The Lincoln-Douglas debates did not at all resemble what we call "presidential debates" today, when a journalist on a panel asks a question and each nominee has a minute or two to answer. In the Lincoln-Douglas debates, one man spoke for an entire hour. Then his opponent spoke for 90 minutes, after which the first speaker had a half hour for rebuttal. Each speaker had the opportunity to respond to all the arguments of his opponent.

The two debaters stuck mostly with a single subject—slavery. Lincoln didn't argue for its abolition. Instead, he focused on the need to ban slavery in the territories. This position offended few in his party and attracted some Northern Democrats. He also exposed the weakness in Douglas's position: Douglas was trying to appeal to both Northern and Southern Democrats.

Lincoln lost the election—just barely. But the debates made him well known throughout the United States. At the same time, Lincoln had harmed Douglas's popularity in both the North and the South.

CHAPTER THREE

The Election of 1860

*A*S THE PRESIDENTIAL ELECTION of 1860 drew nearer, the United States stood on the brink of a crisis. The citizens of its 33 states were bitterly divided. How could any one person hope to lead all Americans?

Because of his debates with Douglas, Lincoln became a leading contender for the Republican presidential nomination. He continued to make himself and his views known throughout 1859, making stirring speeches throughout the Midwest.

In the winter of 1860, he traveled to the East and gave a number of speeches there. In the most notable of these, Lincoln captured national attention once again for his position on slavery: "Wrong as we think slavery is, we can afford to let it alone where it is...

Lincoln captured national attention during his race for the Senate against Stephen Douglas.

but can we, while our votes will prevent it, allow it to spread into the National Territories, and to over-run us here in these Free States?" Citizens had a duty, he said, to stop slavery's spread. He urged, "Let us stand by our duty, fearlessly and effectively."

Of course not everyone agreed with him. The views of the American people were so divided, in fact, that not two, but four political parties took part in the presidential election of 1860. Northerners most-ly supported the new Republican Party.

People in the border states largely supported the Constitutional Union Party. Like the Republican Party, it was a new party. Some conservative Whigs

The Republicans met in Chicago in May 1860 to choose a presidential candidate.

had joined it. So had members of the Know-Nothing Party, which thought the country's problems were caused by immigrants and Roman Catholics.

Most Southerners supported the Democrats. But the Democratic Party split in two when eight Southern states lost a battle over the party platform (the main ideas supported by a party in an election). These states withdrew and decided to run their own candidate for president. They held a separate convention, calling themselves the Southern Democrats.

The winner in this four-way election would have to try to unify a people of vastly different views spread out over a sprawling continent. But none of the four political parties in 1860 represented a majority of the American people. And none of them nominated a presidential candidate at a convention at which all 33 states were represented. The Republican Party was distrusted in the South. Still, it was by then the strongest party in the nation. Its nominee would be in a good position to win the election.

At its convention, the regular Democratic Party nominated Stephen Douglas. The Southern Democrats nominated John Breckinridge, who had been President James Buchanan's vice president. The Constitutional Union Party nominated former Senator John Bell of Tennessee.

The Republican Party met in Chicago in May to choose a nominee. The leader on the first ballot was William Seward of New York. Abraham Lincoln was in second place, followed by Simon Cameron of Pennsylvania, Salmon Chase of Ohio, and Edward Bates of Missouri.

Lincoln gained ground on the second ballot. He

*F*our candidates ran for the presidency in 1860: Stephen Douglas, John Breckenridge, John Bell, and Abraham Lincoln. The Republican convention was held in this building.

THE UNION MUST AND SHALL BE PRESERVED

FREE SPEECH.
FREE HOMES.
FREE TERRITORY.

PROTECTION TO AMERICAN INDUSTRY

FOR PRESIDENT
ABRAHAM LINCOLN
OF ILLINOIS

FOR VICE PRESIDENT
HANNIBAL HAMLIN
OF MAINE

COR. 4TH & CHESTNUT STS. PHILADA.

A Republican campaign poster

was less well known than Seward, but he had fewer enemies and was considered less radical. The supporters of Cameron, Chase, and Bates began switching their votes to Lincoln rather than to Seward; in a sense, Lincoln was everyone's second choice. On the third ballot, Lincoln won the nomination.

His running mate would be Hannibal Hamlin. Hamlin had been governor of Maine and had served in Congress. Strongly opposed to slavery, Hamlin had also helped organize the Republican Party.

In 1860 candidates did not run for president by traveling around the country, shaking hands and giving speeches. Douglas actually broke this "rule" and waged a national campaign. At first, he hoped his campaigning would help him win. Later, he campaigned only in the South, trying to inspire loyalty to the Union.

Lincoln, on the other hand, remained at home in Springfield. He gave only one speech, met with party leaders and with other delegations, and set out his views in a few letters. But many people remembered how Lincoln had discredited Douglas in the debates of 1858. Though Douglas had won that race, the debates had cost him dearly.

On election day, when the votes of the electoral college were counted (the representatives of states who vote for president), Lincoln won. He had a majority of the votes, carrying every free state except New Jersey (which Stephen Douglas won).

But looked at another way, the election had other winners. Breckinridge of the Southern Democrats swept the South, winning the electoral votes of all slave states except Missouri (which Stephen Douglas also won). Three border states were won by Bell.

Lincoln's First Election

CANDIDATE	PARTY	ELECTORAL VOTE	POPULAR VOTE
Abraham Lincoln	Republican	180	1,865,908
Stephen Douglas	Northern Democrat	12	1,380,202
John Breckinridge	Southern Democrat	72	848,019
John Bell	Constitutional Union	39	590,901

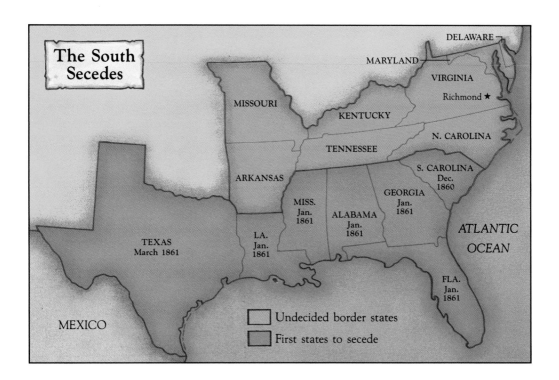

The South Secedes

DELAWARE

MARYLAND

VIRGINIA

Richmond ★

MISSOURI

KENTUCKY

N. CAROLINA

TENNESSEE

ARKANSAS

S. CAROLINA
Dec. 1860

GEORGIA
Jan. 1861

MISS.
Jan. 1861

ALABAMA
Jan. 1861

ATLANTIC OCEAN

TEXAS
March 1861

LA.
Jan. 1861

FLA.
Jan. 1861

MEXICO

Undecided border states

First states to secede

When some Southern states seceded from the Union, several states along the border between North and South wondered whether they should withdraw too.

And Stephen Douglas was not far behind Lincoln in capturing the popular vote. With only 39.9 percent of the popular vote, Lincoln was clearly a minority president. Many Southerners firmly believed that Lincoln represented the best interest of the North alone. And they were not prepared to find out if they were wrong.

Secession Begins

The states of the South prepared to secede, or withdraw, from the nation. It didn't take them long to get organized. In December 1860—just seven weeks after Lincoln's election—a South Carolina convention unanimously declared that "the union now subsisting between South Carolina and the other states, under the name of the 'United States of America,' is hereby dissolved." Meanwhile, James Buchanan was still president of the United States. But when South Carolina seceded, he did nothing but wring his hands.

Five more Southern states followed. Mississippi seceded on January 9; Florida, the next day; Alabama, the next; Georgia, a week later; then Louisiana. On February 4, the six seceding states met in Montgomery, Alabama. They framed a constitution and established a government—the Confederate States of America. Jefferson Davis was elected the Confederate president. For the next few years, the Northern states became known as the Union; the Southern states were called the Confederacy.

Then the Confederacy began open attacks against United States forts. Still, President Buchanan did not respond. Troops from South Carolina, Georgia, Alabama, and Louisiana all seized United States military posts, and Buchanan did nothing. The 15th president of the United States of America said the Constitution did not give the president the power to act.

With six slave states already having left the Union, the other slave states wondered whether they should withdraw too. Eight of them were along the border between North and South: Virginia, North Carolina, Tennessee, Arkansas, Delaware, Maryland, Kentucky, and Missouri. These border states and Texas looked to Buchanan for direction, but looked in vain. In March, Texas joined the Confederacy.

Congress wrestled with the problem of secession in the two months before Lincoln's inauguration. The only compromise the South might have accepted was

President James Buchanan did nothing when the Southern states began to secede.

a return to the Missouri Compromise. But that was unacceptable to Lincoln and the Republicans. A peace convention, chaired by former President John Tyler, met in Washington with Southerners present. No agreement could be reached, however, and the last hope for compromise was dashed.

During these months before his inauguration, Lincoln did not seem to understand how grave the situation was. Also, he showed no willingness to compromise on the central issue—the extension of slavery to the territorites. On this he advised, "Hold firm, as a chain of steel."

And there was something to be said for not making concessions. After all, Lincoln had just won election as president. Why should he back down? He reminded Republican leaders, "We have just carried an election of principles fairly stated to the people. Now we are told in advance, the government shall be broken up unless we surrender to those we have beaten."

Lincoln's uncompromising position made last minute attempts to prevent secession impossible. Thus Lincoln arrived in Washington without having tied his hands or having betrayed the beliefs of his party on the issue of slavery in the territories. But he had done nothing to improve the situation. And no one knew whether he would use force against the seceding states.

By now, Southern officeholders were resigning from the United States government. Rumors of plots to seize control of Washington, D.C., began to circulate. So did rumors of plots to assassinate the president-elect. By Lincoln's inauguration on March 4, 1861, the threats of violence were taken so seriously

Lincoln rode to his inauguration with outgoing President James Buchanan. The dome of the Capitol was under construction.

that the streets of the capital were lined with soldiers. Riflemen were posted on rooftops all along Pennsylvania Avenue. Artillery had been set up at the Capitol.

There a crowd of 25,000 watched an inauguration ceremony full of irony. The 83-year-old chief justice, Roger B. Taney, administered the oath of office. He was the author of the Dred Scott decision Lincoln and his party had criticized so strongly. Meanwhile, Lincoln's old rival, Stephen Douglas, was holding Lincoln's hat (Douglas had reached out to take it when he saw that Lincoln couldn't find a place for it during his inaugural address). In this ironic and violent atmosphere, Abraham Lincoln became the 16th president of the United States.

Lincoln's Qualifications for the Presidency

NSWERING A LETTER FROM AN admirer in 1859, before he became president, Lincoln wrote, "I must say I do not think myself fit for the Presidency." Yet not too many months later, Lincoln admitted, "The taste is in my mouth a little."

On the surface, few men have come to the office of president of the United States less qualified for it than Abraham Lincoln. Compare Lincoln's background with that of the man he followed as president, James Buchanan. Like Lincoln, Buchanan had been a lawyer and a state legislator. But he had also held national office for 23 years (11 in the House of

The boy who grew up in a log cabin moved to the White House when he was 52. He lacked experience in national and international affairs but had other extraordinary abilities.

Representatives and 12 in the Senate). Buchanan also had international experience. He had represented the United States both as minister to Russia and as minister to Great Britain. He had served as secretary of state under President James Polk. In all, Buchanan held national office for 32 of the 36 years before he became president.

Lincoln's experience, on the other hand, was mostly at the state level. He'd held national office for only 2 years—the single term he spent in the House of Representatives. Beyond that, he'd served just 7 years in the Illinois legislature.

Lincoln had no administrative experience at all. He had never supervised a single employee, much less been the governor of a large state (as his Republican rivals Seward and Chase had). And he had no background whatsoever in foreign affairs.

Nor did he have many political connections. Before his campaign for president, he'd never met his running mate, Hannibal Hamlin. He'd never met most of the men who would serve in his cabinet. He was neither widely known nor widely trusted.

Hannibal Hamlin served as vice president during Lincoln's first term.

In addition, Lincoln lacked military experience. Although he would serve as commander in chief during America's greatest war, he had never fought in a war. He had served as a captain in the militia during a brief conflict known as the Black Hawk War, but had seen no action. He had no knowledge of the theory of war. He probably didn't even know how to frame a military order.

Were there any hints at the time Lincoln became president that he might be up to that office? There were two: his ability as a politician and his ability as a communicator.

Though Lincoln had little experience in national office, he knew how to hold his own in the political arena. This cartoon shows him fighting with his rival Stephen Douglas for the White House.

Lincoln was a superb politician. He could get along with people of all kinds. He was good at listening to others, which helped him develop an accurate sense of public opinion. He understood how far ahead of public opinion a leader could be or how far a leader could lag behind it. He knew how to compromise and how to convince others to compromise.

Though he had not held high office for long, Lincoln had over 30 years' experience in politics. His life had been one of "caucuses and conventions, strategems, schemes, and ambitions." He knew how to build party machinery and how to control it. One way was to put together coalitions—temporary alliances of groups with different interests. As a leader in the Republican Party, Lincoln had had to hold together an unwieldy coalition of former members of other parties. These included members of the Whig and Know-Nothing parties as well as radical abolitionists. He knew how to get people of different views to work together.

Like many superb politicians, Lincoln was flexible. He was able to change as events reshaped the political landscape. He needed to be as flexible as possible to deal with changing situations as sensibly as he could. The way things had been done in "the quiet past" would not work in "the stormy present," he told Congress. "The occasion is piled high with difficulty, and we must rise with the occasion. As our case is new, so we must think anew and act anew."

Lincoln also knew how to use patronage—giving jobs in government and politics to allies. And finally, he could withstand political pressure. He was willing to pay the price of criticism over the short term in order to reach a goal.

Lincoln's other great strength was as a communicator. When Lincoln became president, he had not yet given many of his greatest speeches. Still, even in 1861, people knew that the new president was a superb debater and a fine orator. Time after time, he had given speeches of great power.

Many politicians of Lincoln's day spoke and wrote forcefully. They didn't simply read cue cards, but could argue and debate, convince and convert. Even so, Lincoln stood out. Only one other politician, Thomas Jefferson, had written as magnificently as Lincoln. These skills as a politician and communicator would be of enormous value in the White House.

Slavery and the Constitution

When Americans held a convention in 1787 to write the United States Constitution, they needed to compromise on many issues. One of them was slavery. While the words *slave* and *slavery* were not used in the Constitution, acceptance of slavery can be seen in four provisions:

1. Congress was prohibited from ending the importing of slaves until 1808. (Article I, Section 9, Clause 1)

2. The Constitution could not be amended before 1808 to ban the importing of slaves. (Article V)

3. In counting the number of persons for representation in the House of Representatives, "those bound to Service for a Term of Years" were to be counted as three-fifths of other persons. (Article I, Section 2, Clause 3)

4. The states were required to turn over escaped slaves to their owners. (Article IV, Section 2, Clause 3)

Lincoln's Political Principles

What did Lincoln stand for when he became president? He had been a member of the Whig Party, which supported a strong federal government, a government that would help construct roads and canals. He believed that land in the West should be available cheaply to encourage settlement. Lincoln also thought the states should create agricultural colleges. And he believed in higher tariffs—taxes on goods brought into the country.

But what did Lincoln think about slavery? Lincoln hated slavery. But as a practical politician, he accepted the political realities of slavery. Where slavery already existed, it was protected by the United States Constitution; only states could abolish it.

Therefore, nothing could be done about it in the short run.

Though Southerners thought Lincoln was radical, he was not pledged to end slavery—only to keep it from spreading. "The legal right of the Southern people to retain their fugitives I have constantly admitted," he said. The legal right of Congress to interfere with their institution I have constantly denied."

Lincoln believed that slavery would die in time, so long as it was not allowed to spread to new states. He tried to keep it from spreading, arguing that the Constitution gave Congress the power to ban slavery in the territories. He strongly urged Congress to use that power. For his time, Lincoln was not a racist.

But almost to the end of his presidency, he urged blacks to leave the United States and settle elsewhere.

Lincoln's ideas on slavery and black equality changed during the Civil War, as did those of most Americans. He was ahead of public opinion, but he lagged behind the most radical Republicans and abolitionist leaders. For example, William Lloyd Garrison, the editor of a leading abolitionist newspaper, called the United States Constitution a compromise with tyranny. On July 4, 1854, he burned it in protest. Such abolitionists hardly counted Lincoln as one of their own. Indeed, one called Lincoln "the slavehound of Illinois."

The one thing that Lincoln believed in deeply and about which he was not flexible was the Union itself. For Lincoln, the United States represented "the last, best hope" for the survival of liberty in the world. The fight to save the Union would show "the whole family of man" whether a nation "conceived in liberty, and dedicated to the proposition that all men are created equal, can long endure."

Lincoln dedicated the years following his election to winning a terrible war—the Civil War. He fought it to save the Union, convinced that a victory would have lasting significance for the friends of liberty everywhere.

A Civil War drum, *above*, and young soldier, *opposite*. Because Lincoln believed so strongly that the Union must be preserved, the nation began to march to the beat of war when his presidency began.

How Lincoln Made Decisions

*T*HE ONE-TERM CONGRESSMAN who became president in 1861 was about to face the most difficult and agonizing choices any president has encountered. He was keenly aware of his responsibility. When he left his home in Springfield for Washington, D.C., Lincoln compared his own task to that of the country's first president, calling it "greater than that which rested upon Washington."

As president, Lincoln had no one way of making the difficult decisions that arose. He listened a great deal, often did not offer his opinion to those advising him, and took his time deciding. This often gave the appearance of indecision and weakness. In reality, Lincoln withstood a series of crises that would

When Lincoln made decisions, he considered public opinion. He met with many people daily in the White House and at gala receptions such as this one, occasions that he called his "opinion baths."

Detail of a Civil War map

have shattered a weaker man. Others considered Lincoln stubborn and tyrannical. But he met his decisions with humility, courage, independence, and gentleness—if not always with success.

Lincoln was a hard worker. During his administration he rarely left Washington except to make trips to visit his generals and troops in the field—something he felt necessary and also enjoyed. Though he worked hard, he relaxed at times. For example, he spent hot summer nights at the Old Soldiers Home a few miles north of the White House.

At first, Lincoln ran the Civil War with a White House staff of just two secretaries (later it was three). His secretaries were not his advisers, but his aides. They prepared a daily news summary for him, screened his mail and visitors, ran errands, and drafted routine letters. Lincoln not only drafted his more important letters himself, but also wrote out the final copy in longhand. Often he even made another copy for his files; there were no word processors or photocopiers in those days.

Lincoln had an office on the second floor of the White House. He wrote at a table between two high windows. From there, he had a view of the south lawn of the White House, the Washington Monument (only half completed), and the hills of Virginia. Military maps hung on the walls. His desk had pigeonholes where he stuffed correspondence.

Lincoln spent a great deal of time seeing people, many of whom came on personal matters. He held office hours two to four hours a day, seeing members of his cabinet, congressmen, and businesspeople. He also received people seeking jobs for themselves, their family, or their friends.

Lincoln's secretaries tried to protect him from intrusions during the rest of the day so he could work uninterrupted, but they found him difficult to control. They estimated that he spent three-fourths of his time meeting with people. Of the numbers of people who saw him on personal business, Lincoln said, "They don't want much; they get but little; and I must see them." Meeting ordinary citizens also gave him what he called his "opinion baths," when he could get a sense of what the public was thinking.

Lincoln kept his distance from Congress. Congress made a remarkable record while Lincoln was president—passing important banking and currency acts, the Homestead Act, land grants for state colleges, a higher tariff, and approval of a railroad to the Pacific. But Lincoln didn't play an important role in passing these laws. He never tried to be a legislative leader as Thomas Jefferson had been before him and Woodrow Wilson and Franklin D. Roosevelt were after him. In four years, Lincoln vetoed just two bills

Lincoln often traveled on this train to visit his generals and soldiers.

and only pocket vetoed (simply did not act on) another two.

Where the running of the Civil War was concerned, Lincoln was intensely involved—in the choice of generals, with strategy, and even with softening the discipline meted out to soldiers. He made bold use of the powers granted to the commander in chief in the Constitution. Sometimes he took advantage of the times Congress was in recess, making decisions

Lincoln meeting with General William T. Sherman, *left,* General Ulysses S. Grant, *center,* and Admiral David D. Porter, *right.* Lincoln was intensely involved in military decisions during the Civil War.

in their absence. But he was scrupulous in having Congress approve his actions when they met again.

Lincoln's Cabinet

Perhaps one of the most important influences on Lincoln's decisions was his cabinet. As other presidents, Lincoln himself appointed his cabinet—the heads of the Departments of War, Treasury, and State; the attorney general; and other top officials. Lincoln appointed a diverse group, men who often disagreed with him and with each other. Lincoln didn't need "yes men." He could handle and learn from disagreements over major policy questions among his advisers.

Inside and outside the cabinet, Lincoln was criticized for not calling meetings often enough. In fact, Lincoln's cabinet often appeared to be in disarray. This didn't bother Lincoln. He was not a man who believed in organization charts. One of his biographers wrote that he was "an incorrigibly haphazard administrator who seemed oblivious to bureaucratic regulations."

On most of his major decisions, Lincoln consulted members of his cabinet, if not the full cabinet. On some issues, Lincoln consulted his cabinet as a body. For example, Lincoln decided what to do about the siege of Fort Sumter only after a lengthy cabinet deliberation.

On other decisions, Lincoln conferred primarily with one or two cabinet members. He relied most heavily on William Seward, his secretary of state; and Edwin Stanton, his secretary of war. Many of the military decisions of the Civil War were made by Lincoln after conferring with Seward and Stanton.

Lincoln's cabinet in 1861. *Clockwise from top,* William Seward, Salmon P. Chase, Simon Cameron, Montgomery Blair, Hannibal Hamlin, Edward Bates, Gideon Welles, and Caleb Smith. Lincoln's cabinet may have been the strongest in American history. His choices say much about his strengths as president and as a man.

On some matters, Lincoln announced what his decision would be at the beginning of cabinet discussions. But he then went on to ask for advice on timing and on the language with which the decision would be announced.

For the most part, Lincoln left a great deal of discretion to the members of his cabinet in the running of their departments—especially to Secretary of the Treasury Salmon P. Chase, for Lincoln himself knew little about financial matters.

On the other hand, Lincoln intervened in matters of foreign affairs, especially at first. This proved wise because Secretary of State Seward began with some questionable ideas. But as the war went on, Seward steadied, and Lincoln left diplomatic matters more and more to him. This too was wise, for Seward turned out to be one of our great secretaries of state.

To win the war, Lincoln was willing to work with this often contentious group. He was also willing to admit when he had been wrong, something relatively unusual among holders of high office. You can read the memoirs of most modern presidents and not find a single instance when they admit to a mistake.

Abraham Lincoln

Lincoln's signature. Lincoln took responsibility for many difficult decisions himself.

CHAPTER SIX

Lincoln the Man

*L*INCOLN WAS A HUGE MAN FOR his time (Lincoln and Lyndon Johnson, both six-feet-four, were our tallest presidents). He seemed even taller when he wore his stovepipe hat. His head was too small for his body. His ears were large, his neck scrawny, his chest narrow. His eyes were gray and melancholy; his cheekbones high, sunken, and wrinkled. All in all, he looked quite a bit like a scarecrow.

The way Lincoln dressed made him seem even less elegant. The sleeves of his coat were too long, and his trousers were too short. His boots were unpolished, his battered stovepipe hat filled with papers. He didn't grow a beard until just before he became

Lincoln was often brooding and melancholy; he used humor to try to "whistle down sadness."

president. (Lincoln seems to have grown it because an 11-year-old girl suggested he do so.)

In many ways, Lincoln was quite an odd man. He was elected president as "the rail-splitter," the man born in a log cabin who made good. Yet he didn't like to talk about his past and may have been ashamed of some of it (though he had done nothing to be ashamed about). As a frontiersman, he was quite unusual, for he didn't drink, curse, or gamble.

There are more contradictions to be found in Lincoln. He got along well with people and loved companionship. Yet he had few truly close friends, perhaps just one (Joshua Speed, a friend from his earliest years in Springfield). Lincoln's private thoughts were just that—private. He is remembered in part for his deep human sympathy and compassion, yet before he was president he was not known as a man of deep emotions.

One of the most wonderful things about Lincoln was his sense of humor—his love of puns, the superb stories he told, the way he could gently puncture the pompous.

Yet, paradoxically, Lincoln was a sad man always. His life is marked by hints of hopelessness (what would probably be diagnosed now as chronic depression). Though he was realistic and brilliantly logical, Lincoln was also obsessed with signs, visions, dreams, and death.

And there is still one more paradox: Lincoln was not very enthusiastic about organized religion, yet he believed deeply in a God who controlled human destiny.

Perhaps today, with our investigative reporters and all-seeing television cameras, a man with Lincoln's personality might not be taken seriously as a national politician. But things were different in 1860. That was fortunate, because this odd, complicated man turned out to be a great president. And those traits so special to him—his wit, compassion, brooding introspection, tolerance, and kindliness, his absolute lack of pettiness and vindictiveness—marked him as one of the most remarkable of men.

Lincoln's Style

Our great presidents have each had a style of behavior in the highest office that stamped them as unique. George Washington sacrificed his own needs to an all-encompassing dedication to the national interest. Thomas Jefferson combined democratic simplicity with great genius. Franklin D. Roosevelt demonstrated courage so contagious that it lifted and transformed a sick nation. Abraham Lincoln had humility, generosity, compassion, and a wonderful sense of humor, along with his doubts and brooding, his sadness and fatalism.

One of Lincoln's most striking traits was a combination of generosity of spirit and self-control. Enormous demands were made on him as president during the Civil War. At the same time, he had difficulties in his family life. One of his sons, Edward, had died while the Lincolns lived in Springfield. His son Willy died while Lincoln was president, and Mrs. Lincoln was almost crazed with grief. In spite of these pressures, historians have been hard-pressed to discover a single instance when Lincoln showed pettiness, peevishness, arrogance, irascibility, or malice.

Some sense of that spirit can be seen in Lincoln's

Lincoln joked about his height and angular looks. When Stephen Douglas told an audience Lincoln was "two-faced," Lincoln replied, "I leave it to you, ladies and gentlemen. If I had another face, would I wear this one?"

Lincoln with his family, *left to right:* Mary Todd Lincoln, William, Robert, and Theodore. Another son, Edward, died before Lincoln became president. William died in 1862 during Lincoln's presidency.

answer to a long letter from Carl Schurz, a general and a leading Republican. In his letter, Schurz blamed Lincoln for many problems. Lincoln wrote:

> I have just received, and read, your letter....The purport of it is that we lost the late elections, and the administration is failing, because the war is unsuccessful; and that I must not flatter myself that I am not justly to blame for it. I certainly know that if the war fails, the administration fails, and that I will be blamed for it, whether I deserve it or not. And I ought to be blamed, if I could do better. You think I could do better; therefore you blame me already. I think I could not do better; therefore I blame you for blaming me.

Lincoln was sure of himself, sure enough that he could pass off criticism. One of Lincoln's most remarkable traits was the way he did not let his ego get in the way of winning the Civil War. He would, as one scholar said, rather win the war than win an argument. When he was arrogantly snubbed by one of his generals, George McClellan, Lincoln commented, "Never mind. I will hold McClellan's horse if he will bring us success." And when told that Secretary of War Stanton had called him a "damned fool," Lincoln said, "If Stanton said I was a damned fool, then I must be one, for he is nearly always right and says what he means."

Many of Lincoln's critics called him undignified. It is true that Lincoln seems to have had no need to impress. He probably had as little interest in the trappings of the presidency as anyone who has held the office. Of those characteristics which were not at the time deemed presidential, humor was high on the list. The tall president, who towered more than a foot above his wife, was criticized for introducing himself and the first lady as "the long and short of the presidency." Lincoln often read from the books of humorists at cabinet meetings. Chase, in particular, writhed when Lincoln "wasted" the time of the cabinet in this way.

But Lincoln's wit and storytelling served him well with many others. Humor helped him put people at ease, win them over, or sidetrack them when they asked for favors—getting them out of his office without his having to deny their requests. Lincoln also used humor to cheer himself. It helped him "whistle down sadness." This was especially true during the Civil War years, which brought so much pain.

For Lincoln, the White House brought not glory but "ashes and blood." Lincoln had played a role—among other political leaders—in the crisis that led to the Civil War. He must have felt some guilt for that. In addition, he had to shoulder the responsibilities of commander in chief. He knew his choices could bring death to men and grief to their families.

One way in which Lincoln balanced those feelings and found a way to live with himself was through the president's power to pardon. Lincoln knew well the importance of discipline in building a fighting army. Essential to discipline is swift and sure punishment. Yet over and over, Lincoln pardoned soldiers convicted of wrongdoing. He spared men sentenced to death for falling asleep on picket duty, running away during battle, or deserting the army. Signing

one such pardon, he remarked, "I think the boy can do more good above ground than under ground."

Not only did he spare Union boys, but Confederate soldiers as well. For example, Lincoln was asked by the vice president of the Confederacy, Alexander Stephens, if Lincoln could do something for Stephens's nephew, who was a Union prisoner and in poor health. Lincoln gave the boy a parole and sent him home. In return, he asked that Stephens find and parole a Northern boy in similar circumstances. The result: two boys at liberty, one from the Union and one from the Confederacy, both with thanks to Lincoln.

Lincoln felt keen grief over sending men into battle; many were no more than boys, like the young Union soldier above.

The Decision to Fight to Preserve the Union

*W*HEN LINCOLN TOOK OFFICE, THE enormous demands on him began right away. One of the few remaining forts in the South not taken by the Confederates was Fort Sumter, which commanded the harbor of Charleston, South Carolina. But South Carolina troops had the fort surrounded. Union supply ships couldn't get past their guns. The fortress was under siege, slowly being starved out.

The first document Lincoln saw as president was a letter that the commander of Fort Sumter, Major Robert Anderson, had written to Buchanan. The letter held news that shocked Lincoln. Unless they were

Fort Sumter commanded the harbor at Charleston, South Carolina. Confederates opened fire on the fort on April 12, 1861, touching off what may have been the bloodiest war in United States history.

Lincoln's Inaugural Address

*L*incoln put his inaugural address through many drafts. He would speak to a nation in the midst of a crisis, with seven states having already seceded. The address, which he gave on March 4, 1861, offered the South a chance for reconciliation. It could still return peacefully to the Union. "There needs to be no bloodshed or violence," he said, "and there shall be none, unless it is forced upon the national authority."

On the other hand, if the South remained belligerent, the federal government would be forced to act. The South could not secede because the "Union of these States is perpetual," Lincoln said. Nor did it have a right to seize federal forts; the federal government must "hold, occupy, and possess the property and places belonging to the government." Lincoln would use the power confided in him to

enforce that right, but would do only "what may be necessary," he said. Beyond that, "there will be no invasion—no using of force against the people anywhere."

In sum, Lincoln warned the South that it alone could avert a war:

In your hands, my dissatisfied fellow countrymen, and not in mine, is the momentous issue of civil war. The government will not assail you. You can have no conflict, without being yourselves the aggressors. You have no oath registered in Heaven to destroy the government, while I shall have the most solemn one to "preserve, protect, and defend" it.

Abraham Lincoln, the divided nation's new president, was clear. He would do whatever was necessary to preserve the Union.

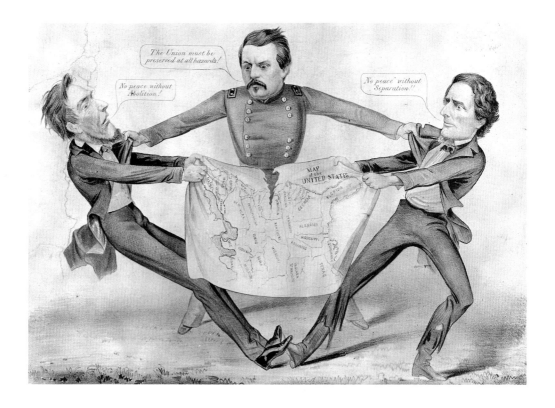

resupplied, Anderson's troops could only hold out for another month.

Lincoln could choose to abandon Sumter. If he didn't want to abandon the fort, he would have to send ships with soldiers and provisions—and risk war. Lincoln had had no idea he would have to make such a crucial decision so quickly.

On March 15, just 11 days after his inauguration, Lincoln gave each member of his cabinet a "homework assignment." "Assuming it to be possible to now provision Fort Sumter, under all the circumstances is it wise to attempt it? Please give me your opinion in writing on the question." Lincoln asked his question without telling the members of the cabinet his own thinking on the question; probably he hadn't yet decided what to do.

This cartoon shows Abraham Lincoln and Jefferson Davis arguing over abolition and secession. Their differences appear to be tearing the country apart. A Union general, George McClellan, warns both: "The Union must be preserved at all hazards!"

When they responded to the question, most of the cabinet members told Lincoln they were against aiding Sumter. Lincoln got five "no" answers, one strong "yes" (from Montgomery Blair, who was postmaster general), and a weaker "yes" (from Secretary of the Treasury Salmon Chase).

Lincoln jotted down on paper the points for and against evacuating Sumter. He appeared to have two choices. The first was to yield, recognizing Southern power over Sumter. The second was to storm in with guns blazing. But if he did that, the Union would appear to be the aggressor. He didn't want to take action that might cause any of the slave-owning states that had not yet seceded to do so.

Later Lincoln said that "all the troubles and anxieties of my life" could not "equal those connected with this decision." For the moment, he chose not to decide. He had four weeks before Sumter would run out of supplies. In the meantime, he sent men he trusted to South Carolina to give him an on-the-spot report as to public feelings about the United States. Because he had chosen not to act, he was criticized in the Republican press for being "indecisive."

When the news from South Carolina came, it was all bad. His messengers could not find any support for the Union. Instead, Lincoln's conciliatory inaugural address was being denounced as a call for war. Once again, Lincoln asked each member of his cabinet to give his opinion in writing, giving them overnight to do so. Lincoln himself stayed up all night.

By dawn of March 29, he had reached his decision. When he announced it to his cabinet, four of them agreed with him. His plan was simple but ingenious. Lincoln would send provisions to Fort

Jefferson Davis was elected president of the Confederate States of America. He believed Southern states had the right to withdraw from the Union.

In the center of these Confederate flags is one reading, "We choose our own institutions!"

States Rights versus Federal Rights

The original 13 colonies thought of themselves as individuals. When they joined the United States of America under one constitution, they took a big step toward thinking of themselves as one. Still, some people continued to think of the states as independent. They thought that since the states had joined the United States voluntarily, they could also choose to leave it.

The United States Constitution gave many powers to the federal government. All powers not specifically named still belonged to the states. The Constitution did not specifically forbid secession, so some people believed the states had a right to secede.

However, the Constitution did say that the federal government could make any laws "necessary and proper" to enforce its powers. Lincoln and others believed this meant the federal government had the right to make the states obey its laws. For this reason, as Lincoln, said, "the Union of these States is perpetual."

Sumter, but not troops. That way the Confederates would have to decide whether or not to start a war.

A week later, thinking about how he could make sure his plan would work, Lincoln had another ingenious idea. He would indeed send provisions, but he would warn the governor of South Carolina that a ship was on its way to Fort Sumter. And he would tell the governor that Union troops would not open fire first.

The Confederates would then have to make a difficult political choice. If they allowed the Union to reprovision Fort Sumter, the new Confederacy would be allowing a "foreign power" to hold a fort dominating one of its major ports. If they didn't, they would have to strike first, a blow against a peaceful ship carrying food.

Lincoln's motives for this plan aren't clear. Perhaps he wanted to "thread his way between war and disunion." Perhaps he simply wanted to convince Northerners that he was doing something. Perhaps he was trying to force the Confederates into firing the first shot. But clearly, he was avoiding an impossible choice—he was neither abandoning Fort Sumter nor starting a war himself.

Lincoln sent the ship. When it arrived in Charleston on April 12, 1861, Confederate troops opened fire. Union troops fired back. Two days later, Major Robert Anderson surrendered to the Confederacy.

The battle had enormous impact. The fort itself was of little military importance, but it had great symbolic significance. The Confederates had attacked a United States fort. Nothing could have united the North more fiercely.

Two days after the Confederates opened fire on Fort Sumter, Major Robert Anderson of the Union surrendered.

Lincoln quickly ordered Union troops to retake the fort, and the Civil War had begun. Three days after the fall of Fort Sumter, Virginia joined the Confederacy. Three more border states—Arkansas, Tennessee, and North Carolina—followed. Eleven states had now seceded from the United States of America.

After the attack on Fort Sumter, the South won the first major victories of the war. Three months later, at the first Battle of Bull Run, Union troops fled in wild disarray to Washington, D.C., nearby. The South's confidence soared. Abraham Lincoln had his work cut out for him.

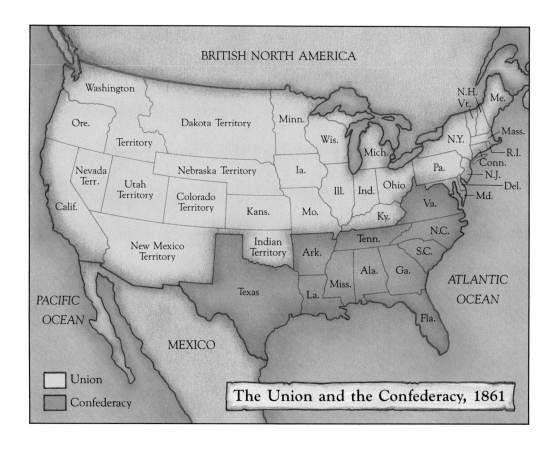

BRITISH NORTH AMERICA

Washington

Ore.

Territory

Dakota Territory

Minn.

Wis.

Mich.

N.H.
Vt.
Me.

Mass.
N.Y.
R.I.
Conn.
N.J.
Del.

Nevada
Terr.

Utah
Territory

Nebraska Territory

Ia.

Pa.

Calif.

Colorado
Territory

Kans.

Mo.

Ill. Ind. Ohio

Va.

Md.

New Mexico
Territory

Indian
Territory

Ark.

Ky.

Tenn.

N.C.

S.C.

PACIFIC
OCEAN

Texas

La.

Miss.

Ala.

Ga.

Fla.

ATLANTIC
OCEAN

MEXICO

☐ Union
☐ Confederacy

The Union and the Confederacy, 1861

Eleven states—including four border states—formed the Confederate States of America in 1861. Twenty-three states (including the new state of Kansas) remained in the Union.

Lincoln and the Constitution

Unlike James Buchanan, Abraham Lincoln had no problem at all finding powers in the United States Constitution to resist secession, nor did he have trouble deciding to use them. Buchanan had believed that the Constitution provided no remedy against secession. Lincoln believed that the Constitution was up to the test of self-preservation. He chose to pursue the war with utmost vigor—pushing his constitutional powers to the limit.

Immediately after the attack on Fort Sumter, Lincoln proclaimed the existence of an insurrection, or armed uprising. Then he took emergency measures. Some of them were actions that only Congress—not the president—has power to do.

First, he called out the state militia and asked for 75,000 volunteers to suppress the insurrection. He also expanded the regular army and navy beyond their legal limits. He closed the post office to "treasonable correspondence." And he directed the spending of two million dollars that Congress had not approved.

Lincoln also set up a blockade of Southern ports. Now the conflict was not just an insurrection. International law said that such a blockade signaled a full-fledged war.

And finally, Lincoln told the commanding general of the armed forces to suspend the writ of habeas corpus. (The writ of habeas corpus is a rule that says government officials can be required to prove in court that a prisoner is being held legally. If they can't, the judge can order the prisoner released). The Constitution says only Congress can suspend the writ of habeas corpus.

Was Lincoln violating the Constitution? He didn't think so. He defended the constitutionality of many of his measures. The Constitution gave the national government these powers, Lincoln argued. Though the powers belonged to Congress, Lincoln said he had acted himself because the emergency had occurred while Congress was not in session.

That was true—but it was not the whole story. After Sumter was attacked, Lincoln had called Congress into a special session. But he didn't seem to be in much of a hurry to see them. He set July 4 as the date the session was to begin—12 weeks after the attack on Sumter.

A Union volunteer

At the beginning of the Civil War, many thought the Union would win easily. It had a far larger population (22 million) than the South (9 million, a third of whom were slaves). It also had a larger army. These Union army wagons were massed at Brandy Station. But in the war's first years, the South won victory after victory.

Lincoln also found the power for many of his wartime actions in those parts of the Constitution that make the president the commander in chief. Those clauses require the president to "take care that the Laws be faithfully executed," and to swear "to the best of my Ability, to preserve, protect, and defend the Constitution of the United States."

Lincoln's actions have been used by later presidents as precedents—setting an example they could follow. For instance, presidents have defended fighting wars without a declaration of war from Congress, or using the army to end strikes.

But Lincoln's situation was unique. He acted only under the most grave circumstances—immediate danger to the nation. Unlike some later presidents, Lincoln didn't need to exaggerate the importance of the situation he faced. He didn't claim to be acting on the basis of secret information only he knew. The danger of war was apparent to everyone.

Lincoln believed deeply in the Constitution and tried to square his actions with it. He wasn't always convincing, but he wasn't cynical or hypocritical either. He believed the Constitution must surely have enough power to preserve itself. When the South seceded, it was violating the Constitution it had sworn to uphold. Enforcing the whole Constitution seemed more important to Lincoln than upholding one fragment of it—a fragment such as the writ of habeas corpus. He wrote: "Are all the laws but one to go unexecuted and the government itself go to pieces lest one be violated?"

When Congress met, it quickly approved Lincoln's measures. The Supreme Court wasn't so sure. Its members were divided about whether or not Lincoln's blockade was constitutional. In the end, they ruled to accept the action as constitutional.

The Decision to Back Down in the *Trent* Affair

*L*INCOLN MADE ONE OF HIS most important decisions during a crisis that came to be known as the *Trent* Affair. He had to decide what to do with two Confederate diplomats the Union was holding prisoner. If he hadn't made a wise decision, the Union might have lost the war—and the Confederacy would have become an independent nation.

On November 8, 1861, Captain Charles Wilkes, commander of the USS *San Jacinto*, deliberately stopped a British ship, the *Trent*. The *Trent* was on its way from Cuba to Great Britain with two Confederate diplomats, James M. Mason and John Slidell, aboard. Mason and Slidell were bound for Europe to seek recognition of the Confederacy. Captain

When the USS *San Jacinto* stopped the British ship the *Trent*, the United States nearly found itself in a war with Great Britain.

Captain Charles Wilkes seized two Confederate diplomats, James M. Mason and John Slidell, on board the *Trent*.

Wilkes, who was not acting under orders, forcibly took the two men off the ship.

Under international law in 1861, a nation at war (like the United States) could stop and search the ship of a neutral country, but only if the commander believed that the ship had contraband aboard. (Contraband is goods that a neutral nation may not supply to a belligerent nation at war.) If Wilkes had found contraband, he should have taken the ship into port so that a court could decide what to do. But Wilkes found no contraband. And he did not seize the ship and take it into port. Instead, he seized the diplomats. This violated Great Britain's rights as a neutral power.

Northerners had had little to cheer about during the first year of the war. So when Wilkes seized Mason and Slidell, they rejoiced, calling the capture a great victory. One observer described their jubilation:

> I do not remember in the whole course of the half-century's retrospect...any occurrence in which the American people were so completely swept off their feet, for the moment losing possession of their senses.

Lincoln was not pleased. He worried that the prisoners might prove to be "white elephants," useless to the Union cause. But for the moment, he remained silent, saying nothing in public of what he thought of the *Trent* Affair.

While Americans exulted over the *Trent* Affair, the British felt outrage. They saw it as an insult to the British flag. The members of the British cabinet believed that Wilkes had been acting under orders, and that the United States was deliberately trying to provoke a war. Ordinary people thought so too. A journalist reported:

> There was never within memory such a burst of feeling as has been created by the news of the boarding.... The people are frantic with rage, and were the country polled, I fear that 999 men of a thousand would declare for immediate war.

And so preparations for war began in Britain. The shipyards were busy night and day to a degree not known since the British had gone to war with Napoleon 60 years before. Some 8,000 troops got ready to sail to Canada, and their fleet was ordered to stand by. Henry Adams, son of the American minister to Great Britain, wrote, "This nation means to make war. Do not doubt it."

Meanwhile, voices of reason on both sides of the Atlantic were urging a peaceful solution. Queen Victoria and her husband, Prince Albert, urged the British cabinet to give the United States a way out while still saving face. The United States could claim that Wilkes hadn't acted under orders; the federal government had never intended to violate international law. Then the United States could simply apologize and return Mason and Slidell.

The British cabinet took this advice and softened the message it sent to the United States. The cabinet reached this decision on December 2—almost a month after Wilkes had boarded the *Trent*. The cabinet couldn't notify Lincoln by telegraph, since the telegraph cable under the Atlantic had recently broken down. Instead, they sent a minister, Lord Lyons, to the United States by ship.

Lyons didn't reach Washington until December 18. By then, tempers had cooled down. Both sides were in a better frame of mind to negotiate. Lord Lyons gave a formal British letter to Secretary of State Seward on December 23. The letter gave the Union one week in which to reply.

Lincoln's cabinet met on Christmas Day to consider the options. Almost no one was convinced that the diplomats had to be released. Lincoln was not sure what to do. Since he'd said nothing in public about the *Trent*, his options remained open, at least to a degree. He didn't want to back down to British threats, but he also didn't want to fight two wars at once. He probably preferred this plan: tell the

Queen Victoria encouraged the British cabinet to use diplomacy to resolve its dispute with the United States.

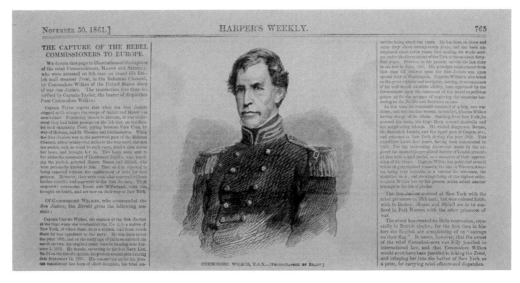

The newspaper above included a portrait of Captain Wilkes in its story on the *Trent* Affair. Journalists in both Britain and the United States reported public outrage over the incident.

British that Wilkes had acted without orders (which, of course, was true). But he wouldn't release the hostages. Instead, the Union and Great Britain would go into arbitration—a process of reaching a solution together.

Two days of discussion produced a different result. At the end of that first day, Lincoln told Seward to make a list of reasons why the Union should release the Confederate diplomats. Lincoln would play devil's advocate. "Now I have a mind to try my hand at stating the reasons why they ought not to be given up," he said. "We will compare points in each side." Both men did this. Seward urged the release of the diplomats. Under international law, he explained, the men had to be given up.

Meanwhile, other cabinet members had come to the same conclusion. Edward Bates argued that "to

James M. Mason, *left,* and John Slidell, *right.* Lincoln eventually released both diplomats, avoiding a war with Britain he could not afford to fight.

go to war with England now is to abandon all hope of suppressing the rebellion." Charles Sumner, chairman of the Senate Committee on Foreign Relations, had been invited to attend the meetings. He also urged the diplomats' release. Reading letters from the Union's strongest supporters in Great Britain, he made an important point. The American cabinet could understand the position of the British cabinet. Like the Americans, they too were under pressure by the public to stand firm and stand up for their country's rights.

Lincoln, on the other hand, did not present his list of reasons to keep the diplomats. When Seward asked him why, the president replied, "I found I could not make an argument that would satisfy my own mind. That proved to me that your ground was the right one." So, in the end, both Lincoln and his cabinet had been impressed by the great risk of war. They also saw that, under international law, the British position was correct.

The only task left was to tell the British what they'd decided. The message would have to satisfy both the British government and the American public. The job fell to Seward. In his message, he admitted that Wilkes had made a mistake. Wilkes should have taken the *Trent* into port so that a court could decide what to do. On the other hand, Seward pointed out that Wilkes was only doing what Britain itself had often done to neutral nations when it was a belligerent. The Union was happy, Seward said, that Great Britain now accepted international law—which was the traditional American position!

The United States never quite apologized, but Seward's letter was good enough. The men were returned. The *Trent* Affair had been a close call, but peace between the Union and Great Britain had survived. The crisis was over.

The Decision Not to Change The Cabinet

*T*WO MEMBERS OF LINCOLN'S CAB-
inet were men of extraordinary ability:
William Seward and Salmon P. Chase.
Though they were brilliant, both men were difficult
to work with. Seward, who was Lincoln's secretary
of state, took office expecting to dominate Lincoln.
Chase, the secretary of the treasury, was ambitious
and self-satisfied.

The cabinet also included the slow-moving Edward Bates as attorney general and the unlikable
Simon Cameron as secretary of war. (Within a year,
Cameron was replaced by Edwin Stanton, upon
whom Lincoln relied heavily.) Montgomery Blair,
postmaster general, was nervous and ill-tempered;
but he was often right on major issues. Gideon

Lincoln's cabinet members often argued with each other and com-
peted with him. *Left to right,* Edwin Stanton, Salmon P. Chase,
Abraham Lincoln, Gideon Welles, Caleb Smith, William Seward
(seated), and Montgomery Blair.

Welles, righteous and puritanical, was an excellent secretary of the navy. Caleb Smith, secretary of the interior, was the least influential of the group.

Four of the seven members of the cabinet were former Democrats. Three, like the president, were former Whigs. Stanton and Chase were from the radical wing of the Republican Party; Seward, Blair, and Welles were more conservative.

All in all, this was a cabinet of strikingly able men who wanted to have things their own way. Virtually no member of the cabinet liked or trusted any other. The radical Chase and the more conservative Seward especially disliked one another.

At the beginning of Lincoln's presidency, none of the cabinet members particularly respected Lincoln, either. Lincoln's old rival Seward seemed to want to run the government. Lincoln gently rebuffed him. Gradually, Seward became a valued adviser and loyal friend to Lincoln.

Edwin Stanton, *left*, Montgomery Blair, *right*, and Gideon Welles, *opposite*

But even after several years with Lincoln, Chase seemed convinced that he could do a better job than Lincoln. He never seemed to stop angling for the presidency. Chase also lacked a sense of humor, and he was jealous of Seward.

Nevertheless, Chase was essential to Lincoln because of his close links to the Republican radicals and because of his immense ability. Chase offered to resign many times, but Lincoln chose not to accept any of his letters of resignation. Instead, he acknowledged Chase's talent, saying, "Chase is about one and a half times bigger than any man I ever knew."

The rivalry between Seward and Chase came to a head in the late fall and early winter of 1862. It was a gloomy time for Lincoln and his party. The Republicans had lost seats in Congress in the midterm elections. Much more seriously, the Union army had been routed at the Battle of Fredericksburg.

Chase, together with Stanton, began complaining to radical Republicans in the Senate. They told the senators that the cabinet was not meeting often enough, and that when it did meet, it was not united. Worse yet, they said, Lincoln was not listening to his whole cabinet but only to Seward, whom they called "the evil genius of the cause."

The radical Republican senators decided that Lincoln should remove Seward from the cabinet. And they thought they could use a recent defeat at Fredericksburg to force Lincoln to do just that. On December 13, 1862, three days after the Battle of Fredericksburg, all 32 Republican senators met secretly. All but one agreed to a plan. They would send 9 delegates to Lincoln. They would ask Lincoln for

The disastrous Battle of Fredericksburg prompted a crisis in Lincoln's cabinet.

"a change and partial reconstruction of the cabinet," so that the cabinet could be made "a unity."

Hearing of this, Seward realized the request was directed at him. He sent Lincoln his resignation. Lincoln immediately walked over to Seward's house (which was near the White House). He told Seward he was sorry that the Republican senators felt as they did. Seward replied that he would be relieved to be free. "That will do very well for you," Lincoln answered, "but...I can't get out."

Lincoln was in a difficult predicament. Chase was a hero to the radicals in the Republican party. Seward was a moderate. Lincoln was closer personally to Seward, but he greatly admired Chase. How could he resist such an overwhelming vote of no confidence from his own party? He decided to try.

Of course, senators should not be running the executive branch. Lincoln could simply have told the senators that it was none of their business. But Lincoln was too shrewd to do that. If he had, he would have had the cabinet he wanted, but he would have lost support in the Congress.

Instead, he invited the senators to talk to him. On the evening of December 18, they met at the White House. He let them speak as long as they wished. He treated them with courtesy, but he said little. Then he invited them to come back the next evening. In the meantime, he met with the cabinet (without Seward being there). He told them what was going on, and asked them to return that evening to meet with the committee.

The senators got there first. They were shocked when the cabinet (again without Seward) filed in. The senators had given Lincoln a memorandum, and Lincoln read it out loud. He discussed the criticisms at length. He said that he had made some decisions on his own responsibility. But, on the most important matters, he had consulted the cabinet. Even though the cabinet sometimes disagreed about particular policies, they all supported the policies once they were decided.

Then Lincoln came to the point. He asked the cabinet, particularly Chase, for their views about the role the cabinet had played. The question put the

Salmon P. Chase is considered to be one of the United States' greatest secretaries of the treasury. He raised money needed for the Civil War and kept the national credit good. He had run against Lincoln for the Republican presidential nomination. While in the cabinet, he continued to covet Lincoln's job.

scheming Chase on the spot. He was in an impossible position. If he said the cabinet was not generally unified once decisions were made, he would not only be lying, but he would be showing his colors as the arch culprit who had started all the trouble. If he agreed with what Lincoln had said, however, he would be contradicting what he had told the senators at other times.

Offended and embarrassed, speaking with hesitation, Chase generally agreed with what Lincoln had said. He agreed that matters of importance had come before the cabinet. Perhaps they had not been discussed "so fully as might be desired," but there had been no want of unity. The senators had lost their ammunition. They could only retreat.

The next morning, the mortified Chase arrived at the White House. Stanton and Welles were present when Chase told the president that he had prepared his resignation.

"Where is it?" the president asked.

"I brought it with me," Chase replied.

"Let me have it." Lincoln took it from Chase and read it. He could not conceal his delight any further. "This cuts the Gordian knot," he said. "I can dispose of this subject now without difficulty. I see my way clear."

Lincoln was not delighted because he wanted Chase's resignation. He didn't want Chase out of the cabinet any more than he wanted Seward out. Now that he had letters of resignation from both men, he could ask both to reconsider and stay in the cabinet. He would not appear to be taking sides. As Lincoln put it, "Now I can ride; I have a pumpkin in each end of my bag."

Lincoln then wrote gentle letters to both men. He refused to let them leave the cabinet, insisting that both were necessary in their places for the war to be won. Both agreed.

And so Lincoln kept his cabinet together. He did so without defying or insulting the Republicans in Congress. He came out of the crisis stronger than before.

As secretary of state, William Seward helped keep European nations out of the Civil War. Lincoln turned down letters of resignation from both Chase and Seward.

The Decision to Free the Slaves

*O*VER AND OVER IN THE SUMMER of 1862, Abraham Lincoln wrestled with the problem of slavery. He hated slavery. But during the early years of the Civil War, Lincoln had several reasons for tolerating it.

For one, he had taken an oath to "preserve, protect, and defend the Constitution of the United States." And surprisingly, the Constitution recognized slavery.

For another, Lincoln didn't think he needed to act to end slavery. Instead, he expected it to die out, especially if it were banned in the territories. He hoped that each state would choose to emancipate, or free, its slaves gradually—first the border states, and then the Confederate states—with the United

Cotton plantations like this one flourished in the South in the 1800s.

$200 REWARD

Ranaway from the subscriber, on Sunday night, the 16th of December, negro boy Gusty, who calls himself GustavusSi mms,he is about twenty years of age, five feet six inches high, dark ginger-bread color, large flat nose, which he almost hides with upper lip when he laughs. He carried away with him one black and one grey coat and a brown over-coat and a pair of drab fulled cloth pants and blue comfort, he also had an oil-cloth clothes bag.

I will pay $50 for his apprehension in the state of Maryland or in the District of Columbia, and $200 if taken in a free State.

ANN P. EVERSFIELD.

Bladensburg Po., Prince George's Co., Md.

If Publishers live on Job Printing office, Husment lot 4th & 7th str., Washington, D. C.

Even before the Civil War, slaves sometimes escaped. United States law said they should be returned to their masters.

States reimbursing owners for the "property" they were losing. Lincoln had been urging this solution to the political leaders of the loyal border states, but they were unenthusiastic.

Another reason Lincoln tolerated slavery at first was public opinion. Most whites in the North were hardly ready to treat blacks with equality. And in the South, people would be enraged if Lincoln ended slavery. Southerners would fight harder than ever.

But perhaps most important, Lincoln didn't want to anger the border states where slavery was legal. These states were loyal to the Union. They might secede if Lincoln emancipated their slaves. Over and over again, Lincoln said that the North was fighting to preserve the Union. To do that, he needed as much help as he could get.

So as the Civil War began, the arguments against emancipation were: It might be unconstitutional. It might be criticized in the North and at the same time make the South fight harder. And it might drive the border states into the arms of the Confederacy.

But as the war went along, some important changes took place. Lincoln weighed the changing circumstances as he thought the problem over.

Lincoln gradually came to believe that he had the constitutional power to free the slaves after all. He could act under his powers as commander in chief, if he could show that emancipation would help to win the war. And it might. For one thing, the South couldn't run its plantations and other businesses smoothly without its slaves.

Also, Union armies began to move onto Southern land. As they did, some slaves were able to flee from their masters. They were freeing themselves. That

presented a problem: What was to be done with these refugees? Technically, they were "fugitive slaves." The law said they ought to be returned to their masters. But surely that was not possible. Besides, the Union armies needed more manpower. Many of the fugitive slaves were joining the Union army. If Lincoln declared them to be free, he could greatly enlarge the Union army.

Lincoln also considered that the first years of the war had brought too few victories and too many humiliations to the North. For example, the Army of the Potomac had withdrawn when it was only a few miles away from Richmond. General George McClellan retreated following a series of attacks by the Army of Northern Virginia under Robert E. Lee. Many believed the Union could have captured the city if it had pressed on.

As Union armies marched through the South, more and more slaves escaped.

Lincoln was also concerned about the possibility of Great Britain or France intervening to try to end the Civil War. The Union had friends in Europe, especially in the working classes. Making the Civil War a war to free the slaves would rally support and make it more difficult for the European governments to intervene.

At home, public opinion began to change. Abolitionist sentiment in the North grew as the war progressed. By the summer of 1862, Lincoln felt constant pressure from the radicals in his party to deal the death blow to slavery.

Finally, Lincoln came to see that the solution he favored was not going to work. On July 12, 1862, he gave congressmen from the loyal border states one last chance. He presented a plan in which the federal government would reimburse slave-holders for their slaves. But the congressmen rejected his proposal, voting 20 to 9 against it. If congressmen from loyal border states wouldn't agree to give up slavery under such generous terms, surely leaders in the South would never agree. Slavery was not going to die a natural death.

The next day Lincoln told Seward and Stanton that he'd made a decision: He would order that all slaves in the South were free. That would be an extraordinary move. But extraordinary measures were necessary, he thought, to preserve the Union. "We had about played our last card," Lincoln later explained, "and must change our tactics, or lose the game!"

Then, on July 21 and 22, Lincoln discussed the matter with the whole cabinet. Only Stanton and Bates were sure Lincoln's decision was the right one.

Blair was concerned that public opinion had not shifted enough. The decision might cost Lincoln the fall election. Chase was unexpectedly cautious.

But it was Seward who made the most convincing argument. He urged Lincoln not to announce his decision right away. It might look like an act of desperation. Instead, Lincoln should wait until the Union had won an important military victory. That

Lincoln decided not to announce emancipation until the Union won a major victory. A Southern slave woman, *above,* waits as Confederate soldiers in the background bring in Union prisoners after yet another victory.

way, Seward said, it would be "borne on the bayonets of an advancing army, not dragged in the dust behind a retreating one."

Lincoln agreed. He had already begun working secretly on the document that would announce his decision: the Emancipation Proclamation. He wrote at a table in the office of the Superintendent of the Military Telegraph, where he often went to find out the latest war news. Now, reluctantly, he put the proclamation away.

As it turned out, the Union army did not win a "major victory" for another two months. During that time, no one knew of the Emancipation Proclamation. The cabinet members were able to keep it secret. And the president gave no hints of it through his public statements—at least, if they were not read very carefully. For example, in August he wrote the influential editor, Horace Greeley:

> My paramount object in this struggle is to save the Union and is not either to save or destroy slavery. If I could save the Union without freeing any slave I would do it, and if I could save it by freeing all the slaves I would do it; and if I could do it by freeing some and leaving others alone I would also do that.

His last phrase summed up his position—if he could save the Union by freeing some slaves but not others, he would. But he was not ready to admit it. Then, on September 13, Lincoln told a group of religious leaders, "I have not decided against a proclamation of liberty to slaves." But the time was not yet right. If he proclaimed the slaves free, he would do so out of strength, not weakness. Emancipation

should not appear to be a desperate measure to win the war. "What good would a proclamation from me do…as we are now situated?" he asked.

The major victory Lincoln needed came when the Union army stopped Robert E. Lee's Confederate Army of Northern Virginia at Antietam. Lincoln called a cabinet meeting for September 21, 1862. The cabinet members all knew the meeting would be important. Even so, Lincoln opened the meeting by reading a chapter from a book by Artemus Ward, a humorist. But then he made a serious announcement. "When Lee came over the river," he said, "I made a resolution that if McClellan drove him back, I would send the proclamation after him."

Now he was prepared to do just that. He did

The Battle of Antietam. If the Union army could drive back Confederate General Robert E. Lee at Antietam, Lincoln said he would "send the proclamation after him."

The Emancipation Proclamation made the Civil War a war to end slavery.

not wish the cabinet's advice "about the main matter—for that I have determined for myself." He had already considered each of their views on whether and when to issue the proclamation as thoroughly as he could. Instead, he asked them only to consider "the expressions I use" and other minor points.

He would shoulder the responsibility for the proclamation. With his unique blend of humility and self-confidence, he said, "I know very well that many others might, in this matter, as in others, do better than I can." But Lincoln alone was president. "I am here," he said. "I must do the best I can, and bear the responsibility of taking the course which I feel I ought to take."

At last, on September 22, 1862, Lincoln took the first public step. He issued a preliminary proclamation. It warned the Confederacy that it must return to the Union by January 1, 1863. If not, Lincoln would proclaim its slaves to be free.

The preliminary proclamation infuriated the South. No Southern state returned to the Union. When New Year's Day arrived, Lincoln did not hesitate. Without any special ceremony, he signed the final Emancipation Proclamation the same day. He was sure of his decision—so sure that he told Seward, "I never in my life felt more certain that I was doing right, than I do in signing this paper."

Oddly, though, the decision did not have an effect right away. The Emancipation Proclamation did not by itself free a single slave. It applied only to areas in the South where the Union armies were not in control.

Nonetheless, it had an enormous impact, strengthening the Union's position. For one thing, it gave

hope to slaves throughout the South. More and
more escaped. Many of those served in the Union
armies—nearly 200,000 by the end of the year—
adding manpower the Union needed. Also, while
some in the North criticized the proclamation, on
the whole it did stimulate new enthusiasm for the
war effort.

Some Europeans also criticized the proclamation. *The Standard,* a London newspaper, called it
"a sham," "the wretched makeshift of a pettifogging

Many African Americans
served courageously in the
Civil War, including nearly
200,000 former slaves.

A slave family listens as a Union soldier reads the Emancipation Proclamation in their cabin.

lawyer." But overall, the proclamation also helped the Union in Europe. Just as Lincoln had expected, the proclamation made it almost impossible for European nations to intervene in the war. They could hardly interfere in a fight against slavery.

The Emancipation Proclamation bolstered the Union, but it also bolstered the South. Southerners saw that the Union was now fighting for a goal that would change life in the South completely. So the

South dug in its heels—it would fight on until it was completely defeated.

At many times during the Civil War, Lincoln's decisions were influenced by circumstances beyond his control. As he said, "I claim not to have controlled events but confessed plainly that the events have controlled me." Circumstances affecting this decision included military setbacks, escaping slaves, and the unwillingness of the border states to accept gradual emancipation.

But Lincoln did have some control. Public opinion early in 1862 would have made the Emancipation Proclamation politically impossible then. Then sentiment in the North slowly changed. What was not possible in January was possible in July or September. By being flexible, Lincoln was able to take advantage of that change.

Lincoln had decided the timing and the manner of the proclamation shrewdly. He had lagged behind the abolitionists, but he had moved out ahead of the rest of public opinion in the North. He waited long enough for emancipation to work.

Late in 1864, Lincoln took emancipation one step further. He put great pressure on wavering members of Congress to adopt what became the Thirteenth Amendment to the Constitution—the amendment that abolished slavery.

In the end, Lincoln came to see that emancipation was "the central act of his administration." In fact, it may well have been the greatest event of the nineteenth century.

Decisions in Finding a General

W HEN THE CIVIL WAR BEGAN, THE
Union had many advantages over the Confederacy. It had many more people and so
could gather larger armies. It had far more industry,
producing the goods and money it needed to fight
a war. And it had better rail transportation.

But the Union had some disadvantages too. It had
few trained officers and no great generals. The head
of the Union armies was Winfield Scott, a hero of
the Mexican War. Scott was 75 years old and had
many ailments. He wasn't up to active command.
And Lincoln was ill prepared for war. He had no
military training. He had little experience—he had
been a captain in the militia during the Black Hawk
War, but had seen no action.

General Ulysses S. Grant and his men. Lincoln's search for a brilliant general ended when he began to notice Grant.

The Confederacy had formidable military leaders, including President Jefferson Davis, *seated,* and General Robert E. Lee, *fourth from right.*

On the other hand, the Confederacy had strong military leaders. Most of the leading generals (such as Robert E. Lee) decided to fight for the Confederacy. In addition, the president of the Confederacy, Jefferson Davis, seemed ideally suited to be a wartime leader. He had been trained at West Point and had been United States secretary of war.

Though Lincoln didn't have the background that Davis did, he turned out to be a superb wartime leader too. He became an excellent military strategist. He learned all he could by reading, spending many nights with books on military strategy. He drew up strategic plans and made military policy.

The Union's railroads, steamships, and telegraph lines were superior to the Confederacy's. Perhaps better than anyone, he realized the significance of this. Together with the Union's larger armies, these assets revolutionized the nature of war. He saw that the Union should use its larger armies and superior transportation and communication to attack the Confederate armies at all points at the same time. That would make it impossible for the Confederacy, which had fewer troops, to move troops from one threatened point to another. A breakthrough somewhere would become inevitable.

Sometimes, Lincoln even directed tactical movements, ordering where and when an army should move. Many modern presidents rely on their top military advisers, the joint chiefs of staff, for such decisions. But Lincoln made many military decisions himself.

For example, Lincoln visited Fortress Monroe in southern Virginia in the spring of 1862. The army wanted to invade Norfolk, Virginia, by sea and needed a secure place to land. Lincoln steamed up and down the coast looking for a good spot. When he found one, he personally directed the attack (the commanding general was away) that led to the occupation of Norfolk. In all, Lincoln left Washington 11 times to visit the Union's Army of the Potomac in Virginia and Maryland, spending 42 days with them.

Lincoln struggled through many unhappy times

as commander in chief. He watched from the White House as Union soldiers made their frantic retreat from Bull Run. He spent hours agonizing at the telegraph office. And he watched Union and Confederate men die in battle.

Sometimes Lincoln's own life was in danger. One day in July 1864, Confederate cavalry reached Fort Stevens on the outskirts of Washington, D.C. Lincoln went to watch the fighting. One young soldier, seeing Lincoln standing on a low wall, yelled at him, "Get down, you damn fool, before you get shot." That young soldier was Oliver Wendell Holmes Jr., a war hero, who became one of the great justices of the Supreme Court of the United States (and who would live until Franklin D. Roosevelt became president).

Lincoln knew the Union needed "slugging, driving generals" who wouldn't let up, so that the North could take advantage of its edge in manpower, weapons, and transportation. Yet Lincoln chose general after general not up to the job. General Henry Halleck, who was named supreme commander, had all the right credentials. But he hated to give orders. General Irwin McDowell was routed at Bull Run. General Ambrose Burnside used a disastrous strategy at the Battle of Fredericksburg. General John Pope was conceited and hated by his troops. General Joseph Hooker had a problem too; he couldn't get along with Halleck.

Most exasperating of all was the handsome and magnetic General George McClellan. McClellan was superb at training armies and was adored by his troops. But he found every possible excuse to put off fighting. He got within 20 miles of Richmond

After the Battle of Bull Run in July 1861, Lincoln appointed George McClellan the commanding general of Union troops. McClellan was superb at training an army but cautious in using it.

Civil War Time Line

YEAR	DATE	EVENT
1860	December 20	– South Carolina secedes.
1861	March 4	– Lincoln is inaugurated.
	April 12–14	– Confederates take Fort Sumter.
	July 4	– Lincoln asks approval of emergency actions.
	July 21	– Confederacy wins First Battle of Bull Run.
	December 28	– Cabinet resolves *Trent* Affair.
1862	May–July	– McClellan advances on Richmond, waits for reinforcements, and retreats.
	September 17	– Union wins Battle of Antietam.
	September 22	– Lincoln announces preliminary Emancipation Proclamation.
	December 10	– Union defeated at Fredericksburg.
	December 13	– Senators demand Seward's resignation.
1863	January 1	– Lincoln issues Emancipation Proclamation.
	July 1–3	– Union wins Battle of Gettysburg.
	July 4	– Grant's troops take Vicksburg, Mississippi.
1864	March 9	– Grant takes command of all Union troops.
	September 2	– Sherman occupies Atlanta, Georgia.
1865	April 9	– Lee surrenders to Grant.

Lincoln visiting McClellan at Antietam.

in the spring of 1862 with Union forces that could easily have overwhelmed the Confederates. But he didn't enter the Confederate capital. Instead, he waited for reinforcements—and lost his opportunity to take the city. Later, at the Battle of Antietam, McClellan failed to pursue the Confederate army led by Robert E. Lee. It escaped to Virginia.

"He has the slows," Lincoln said of McClellan.

Lincoln came closer to being irritable with McClellan than with anyone else during the war. At one point Lincoln wrote McClellan, saying that if McClellan did not intend to use the army, he would like to "borrow it." At another time, replying to still another McClellan excuse, Lincoln cabled:

> I have just read your despatch [sic] about sore tongued and fatigued horses. Will you pardon me for asking what the horses of your army have done since the battle of Antietam [five weeks before] that fatigue anything?

Some Republicans in Congress recognized McClellan's weakness and called for his resignation. At first, Lincoln ignored them and stuck by McClellan. But finally Lincoln realized McClellan couldn't fight—and removed him.

Why did Lincoln choose such a motley crew of generals? Mainly, because better men were not available. In addition, some of Lincoln's choices were the result of his lack of military experience. He appointed generals recommended to him by generals, members of Congress, and state governors. Lincoln learned, however. He came to see what kind of generals the Union needed.

As the war progressed, Lincoln watched one little-known soldier, Ulysses S. Grant, with interest. Lincoln appreciated Grant's talents, and finally made him commanding general. Grant then came up with a brilliant plan to win the war. Ironically, Grant's plan closely resembled the one Lincoln had tried to sell to his generals earlier.

Grant often drew criticism, but Lincoln stood firmly behind him. For example, Lincoln was told

In 1863, the tide began to turn in the Union's favor. On July 4, Ulysses S. Grant won an enormous victory at Vicksburg, Mississippi. By then Robert E. Lee and his army had pushed into Pennsylvania, but they were decisively defeated at Gettysburg. In the fall, by winning the battle of Chattanooga (Lookout Mountain), the Union won control of the Mississippi River, splitting the South in two.

During the summer of 1864, Union General William T. Sherman invaded Georgia with an army of 100,000. They occupied Atlanta and then marched to the sea, destroying factories, warehouses, and railroads on the way.

that Grant had been drinking during battle (he hadn't). The president answered, "Find out the name of his brand so I can give it to my other generals." When Grant was bitterly criticized for the losses he took at the Battle of Shiloh and there were cries for his removal, Lincoln said, "I can't spare that man. He fights."

As Grant distinguished himself, the officers under him also did well. Lincoln was finally able to put a winning team on the field in 1864: Ulysses S. Grant as general in chief of all the Union armies, Henry

Halleck as chief of staff (where he didn't have to give orders), and William T. Sherman as commander in the West.

Lincoln contributed significantly to the Union's final victory in three important ways. First, he spotted Grant's talents and protected him from his critics. Second, Lincoln was far ahead of his generals and advisers in realizing the best Union strategy. Third, Lincoln also understood the importance of damaging the economy of the South. Emancipating slaves and encouraging them to flee harmed the South's economy. So did the march of Sherman's army through Georgia, wrecking factories, slaughtering cattle, and carrying off crops. This tough strategy drained the South of precious resources.

The weaknesses of Lincoln's early generals no doubt lengthened the Civil War. Lincoln was a gentle man who chose to fight a hard war so that he could make a gentle peace. He kept after his generals constantly to fight. Even at the very end, he wired Grant, "General Sheridan says, 'If the thing is pressed I think Lee will surrender.' Let the thing be pressed." In these ways, Lincoln finally overcame all the poor generalship of the early years of the war.

Ulysses S. Grant took charge of all Union troops in 1864. Grant's appointment was one of the key decisions of Lincoln's presidency.

Final Days

*O*N APRIL 14, 1865, THE AMERICAN
flag was raised once again over Fort Sumter.
It was raised by Major Robert Anderson, the
commander who had surrendered it almost exactly
four years before. In those terrible years of war,
600,000 Union and Confederate lives had been lost.

The weeks before that event had probably been
the happiest of Lincoln's presidency. Reelected president in 1864, he was inaugurated for the second
time on March 4, 1865. By then, Union armies had
surrounded and taken the Confederate capital at Richmond, Virginia. The Union occupation of Richmond
was an important indication that victory for the
North was near.

Lincoln decided to visit the city with his son Tad.

On April 2, 1865, Robert E. Lee evacuated Richmond. A week
later, Lee surrendered to Grant at Appomattox Court House.

When they arrived, crowds of freed slaves poured into the streets to pay Lincoln tribute. Lincoln was asked by the Union general in Richmond how to treat the people he had just conquered. Lincoln replied, "If I were in your place, I'd let 'em up easy, let 'em up easy."

Then Lincoln received the news that Robert E. Lee had surrendered. Lee's surrender marked the beginning of the end for the Confederacy. When Grant asked Lincoln about the terms for Lee's surrender, Lincoln was generous again. He replied, "Give them the most liberal terms. Let them have their horses to plow with, and...their guns to shoot crows with. I want no one punished."

Above left, the evacuation of Richmond. *Left*, Lincoln rides into Richmond in triumph. The painting probably exaggerates Lincoln's reception. It is likely that few whites in Richmond greeted him.

When Lincoln was inaugurated for the second time, his vice president was a Democrat—Andrew Johnson. Lincoln had not asked Hannibal Hamlin to run with him again on the Republican ticket. Lincoln wanted a Democrat on the ticket, one of many ways Lincoln sought to reunite the nation.

Soon other Confederate forces surrendered as well. The Union had won the war, and crowds came to the White House to hail Lincoln. Lincoln spoke to his wife of a more peaceful second term and, afterwards, quiet retirement in Illinois.

But before he could retire, Lincoln faced yet more difficult decisions. Now that the Union had won, what should happen next? It would not be easy to create a plan for reconstruction—the rebuilding of the nation.

During the war, Lincoln had announced a plan that gave the South liberal terms for readmission to the Union. But that plan was designed to entice individual states to stop fighting and rejoin the Union. In 1864, Congress passed a harsher plan, which Lincoln allowed to die by pocket veto.

With the collapse of the Confederacy in 1865, the situation was completely different. On his last full day as president, Lincoln and his cabinet discussed reconstruction. He said he wanted the South to get up and running as quickly as possible. "If we were wise and discreet," he told them, "we should reanimate the states and get their governments in successful operation."

After making a plan for reconstruction, Lincoln would have to "sell" it to the radical Republicans, to the more moderate Republicans and Democrats in the North, and to the South. The next difficulty would be enforcing the plan. But at least the war was over. The North rejoiced, and so did Lincoln.

Underneath Lincoln's happiness, however, something troubled him. He told several people, including his wife, about a dream that he had had. In the dream, he heard sobbing. He walked from room to room in the White House until at last he arrived at the East Room. There he saw soldiers on guard surrounding a catafalque (the raised structure upon which a coffin rests at a state funeral).

"Who is dead in the White House?" Lincoln asked.

"The president," came the answer. "He was killed by an assassin."

From the day of his election, Lincoln had always walked in the shadow of death. He found that theater, concerts, and opera gave him relief from his burdens. Still, he had not wanted to go to Ford's Theatre on the night of April 14, 1865. He did so to please his wife. He had hoped that General Grant and his wife would be with them, but those plans had fallen

Ford's Theatre as it looked during Lincoln's presidency

Five days after Lee's surrender, Lincoln was shot by
John Wilkes Booth.

through. Delayed at the White House, the president
arrived late for the play. The band struck up "Hail
to the Chief," and the audience rose and cheered him.

Then came a bullet from John Wilkes Booth. The
bullet struck one of the few people who had never
given way to hate in a time when millions had hated.
Lincoln was carried across the street. Stanton and
Welles and other members of the cabinet, Vice President Johnson, Mrs. Lincoln, and Lincoln's oldest son,
Robert, came to Lincoln's side. The president barely lived through the night. By early morning, he
was dead.

Two days after the killing, Lincoln's body was brought to the White House. Lincoln lay in state dressed in the black suit he had worn when he had first addressed the nation as president. A huge throng, perhaps 25,000, filed past in two columns to say good-bye to their wartime leader. The next day many important people gathered in the White House's East Room for the funeral. The president's two sons, Robert and Tad, were there, but Mrs. Lincoln was too upset to attend.

Then Lincoln's body was moved from the White House to the Capitol to lie in state for one more

Lincoln died surrounded by cabinet members, Mrs. Lincoln, and his son Robert.

day. To the muffled beat of drums, gunfire from the forts surrounding the capital, and the tolling of church bells, the saddest procession in American history moved up Pennsylvania Avenue. Bands played mournful music. Six gray horses drew a black hearse. A riderless horse followed. Then came people—about 40,000. Wounded soldiers—some who left hospital beds, some on crutches, some with bandages—made their way up the avenue. So did at least 4,000 black

Americans, walking in lines of 40 from curb to curb, holding hands as they proceeded.

A week after the assassination, a funeral train took Lincoln's body home to Springfield, Illinois. Along the way, hundreds of thousands of mourners waited and watched in silence as the train passed by. Even in Baltimore, a city that had joined the Confederacy, tens of thousands came. On the night run from Columbus to Indianapolis, bonfires lit the route. In Chicago, 10,000 school children wearing black armbands marched with the coffin. Finally, in Springfield, Lincoln was buried at Oak Ridge Cemetery.

It was too late now for Lincoln to unveil a plan for the reconstruction of the South. It would not be for him to decide whether to "Let 'em up easy, let 'em up easy." America's 16th and probably greatest president, Abraham Lincoln, belonged to the ages.

Opposite, Lincoln's funeral procession in Washington, D.C. *Above,* the black hearse that carried the fallen president.

The Last Great Decision: How to Reconstruct the South

*A*BRAHAM LINCOLN DID NOT LIVE to make a last great decision—the decision about how to reconstruct the South. It was probably as important as the decisions to preserve the Union and to free the slaves. Any plan for reconstruction had to balance two important goals: the reunion of the nation and meaningful liberty for black Americans.

Many questions about reuniting the nation had to be answered. What would the Union require of the states that had seceded? Would the South be punished? Or taken back into the Union freely? What about its leaders—should they be punished, and if so how? What would be required of the vast

Rebel soldiers sadly roll up the flag of the Confederacy. Lincoln felt grief for their losses. After discussing peace terms with the president, Admiral David D. Porter wrote, "His heart was all tenderness."

The Civil War killed more than 600,000 Union and Confederate soldiers.

majority of white Southerners who had been loyal to their states?

Questions about the treatment of freedmen (the newly freed slaves) also needed answers. By the end of the Civil War, these included not only slaves in the South, but also in the North. What rights did they have? What must the United States government do to make sure that their rights were protected?

Lincoln had been deeply committed to both of the goals that had to be balanced. He had wanted speedy reunification of the nation on generous terms. He had also wanted the rights of the freedmen meaningfully protected.

After Lincoln's death, Vice President Andrew

Johnson became president. Johnson fought hard for a program of reconstruction that placed national unity over black equality. Congress did not support Johnson's approach. They wanted to treat the freedmen better and the South more harshly. Eventually, Johnson was impeached, or charged with misconduct. He was almost removed from office by Congress. So in the short run, it was Congress's policy that won out.

By 1877, however, the nation had tired of reconstruction. The United States government got out of the business of protecting the rights of the freedmen, leaving them to the mercies of the white South. The result was the system of segregation and inequality that lasted for some 90 years after the Civil War ended.

Could Lincoln have done better? Of course, no one knows for sure. Lincoln had fought the war hard. He approved Sherman's savage march through Georgia. Even when Grant's victory seemed certain, he told him to hold on "with a bulldog's grip." By the end of the war, the cities of the South lay in ruins.

As victory came closer, he had moments of elation. Even more, he felt deep sadness. He knew well of the four years of suffering and death for both sides.

Lincoln never felt that only one side was right. He didn't forget that the object of the war had been to preserve the Union. A few days before he died, a band played Union marching songs for him. Lincoln told them he also wanted to hear "Dixie"—the song of the Confederacy.

Lincoln never wanted revenge. Just as he was never petty in his personal dealings, he never spoke vindictively about the South. During the war he gave pardons to soldier after soldier. After the war, he intended to forgive the South as a whole.

Lincoln stated those views most eloquently in the concluding lines of his second inaugural address:

> With malice toward none; with charity for all; with firmness in the right, as God gives us to see the right, let us strive on to finish the work we are in; to bind up the nation's wounds; to care for him who shall have borne the battle, and for his widow, and his orphan—to do all which may achieve and cherish a just, and a lasting peace, among ourselves, and with all nations.

Lincoln knew the rights of freedmen such as this soldier would need protection after the war.

But how far would Lincoln have gone to protect the rights of the freedmen? We cannot be sure, for just as Lincoln's views on emancipation had changed during the war, so his views on equality were changing, as he saw that things which were once impossible to achieve became possible.

Lincoln had viewed slavery as part of a greater problem—keeping the Union together. Still, Lincoln was probably more sympathetic to the problems of black Americans than any president would be until the 1960s. He believed deeply that all white Americans shared guilt for slavery. And he believed that the war was the punishment God had inflicted on the United States for having had such a system.

Three days before he was shot, Lincoln gave his last speech from the balcony of the White House. He cautiously supported giving freedmen the right to vote—at least those who were "very intelligent and those who had served the Union as soldiers." Although the views of his countrymen had changed during the war, Lincoln knew that an even greater

The Civil War left the South in ruins. Lincoln fought the war hard, but he hoped to make a gentle peace.

change was necessary for further movement toward racial equality.

So what might have Lincoln decided about reconstruction? He would not have supported harsh treatment of the South nor of the Confederate leaders. He would have supported rapid readmission of the Southern states to the Union.

Where the rights of the freedmen were concerned, Lincoln would probably have moved cautiously forward, avoiding commitments until public opinion had gotten closer to where he stood privately. He probably would have expected to keep the Union army in the South for a while to protect the interests of the freedmen. Lincoln recognized the racism that existed in the South and in the North. He would

The Thirteenth Amendment being passed in the House of Representatives

have supported policies that were steps along the road to justice and to racial equality.

Lincoln's Legacy

The Civil War caused more death and destruction than any war of the nineteenth century. By its end, as one historian said, "Slavery was dead, secession was dead, and 600,000 men were dead." The war decided forever that the Union was supreme over the states. As a result of the war, Southern influence on the federal government gave way to that of Northern and Midwestern Republicans.

Three new amendments to the Constitution resulted from the war: The Thirteenth Amendment freed the slaves; the Fourteenth Amendment said that no state "shall deprive any person of life, liberty, or property without due process of law, nor deny to any person equal protection of the laws." The Fifteenth Amendment barred discrimination in voting.

Although all three amendments had been added to the Constitution to help protect the former slaves, they didn't work out that way. For many years blacks were prevented from voting in the South. For many years the Fourteenth Amendment was used to protect property rights, not civil rights. It was not until the 1950s that the Supreme Court, led by Earl Warren, finally interpreted the Fourteenth Amendment as it had been intended. Spurred by civil rights demonstrations, Presidents John F. Kennedy and Lyndon B. Johnson and the Congress began a second reconstruction to try to fulfill the promise of equality. This is part of the legacy of Abraham Lincoln.

So is the strong presidency of the twentieth century. Theodore Roosevelt, Woodrow Wilson, Franklin Delano Roosevelt, and later presidents all found in the Constitution language permitting the president to take strong actions to protect the public at home and the national interest abroad. When they took these actions, they pointed out that it was Lincoln who first found in the Constitution such broad presidential powers.

President Lincoln had to make some of the most difficult decisions any president has faced. Some were handled brilliantly—the *Trent* Affair, the confrontation with Congress over the makeup of the cabinet. In some decisions, Lincoln was driven by events, but was able to shape the result through the way he acted or through his timing. Fort Sumter and the Emancipation Proclamation are examples of this. With still other decisions—as in his choice of generals—Lincoln was no better than the material he had to work with.

When the Thirteenth Amendment was passed, onlookers in balconies of the House of Representatives cheered and applauded. Believing slavery to be dead, abolitionist leader William Lloyd Garrison urged the American Anti-Slavery Society to close. But the fight for civil rights by African Americans continued for many years.

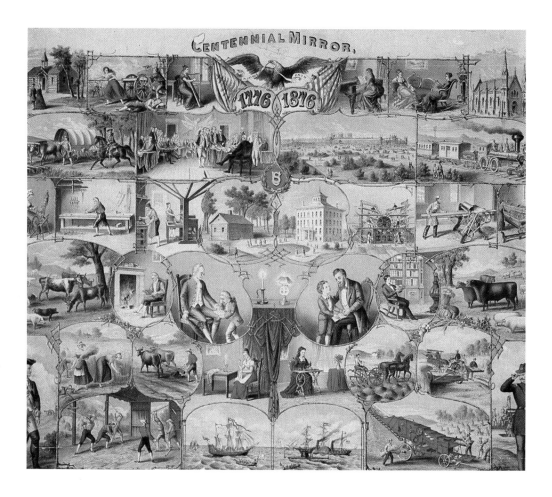

This centennial poster shows progress in the United States in its first 100 years, from 1776 to 1876. Lincoln left a rich legacy to a nation struggling toward its second century.

Abraham Lincoln combined stubborn courage with flexibility, independence with the ability to compromise, realism with great vision. He helped preserve the Union. He freed the slaves. And he knew what the struggle in America meant to people everywhere in the world. Remember what he said at Gettysburg: Our fathers had brought forth "a new nation conceived in Liberty and dedicated to the proposition that all men are created equal." The Civil War was testing "whether that nation, or any nation so conceived and so dedicated, can long endure." Or as he said at another time, "We shall nobly serve, or meanly lose, the last best hope on earth." What might have died with secession was the hope America had given to people all over the world—a land of freedom and opportunity.

But Lincoln's greatness goes even beyond this vision of a better world for millions of people he didn't know. Not all great men are admirable men. Lincoln was. He cared not only about people in general, but also about people in particular. Under the most difficult conditions he was compassionate and tolerant to those around him and those who came to him. He remained patient with those who besieged him for jobs and favors. He made the time to hear about the ill Confederate soldier and the deserter from the Union army, and he cared genuinely enough to help them.

Of all our presidents, Abraham Lincoln was the one least spoiled by his great office. He probably was our greatest president, although George Washington and Franklin Delano Roosevelt come very close. But he was certainly the most noble man—more so even than Washington or Thomas Jefferson—to serve as president of the United States.

This is believed to be the last portrait of Lincoln's life. Lincoln was a noble man, perhaps the most noble ever to serve as president of the United States.

Index

Acknowledgments

Photographs reproduced with permission of: Chicago Historical Society, pp. 2, 47, 68, 116; Independence National Historical Park, p. 6; National Archives, pp. 8 (above), 119, 126, 129; IPS, pp. 8-9 (below), 11 (both), 24, 55, 58, 94, 108; James Graham and Sons, NYC, p. 12; Library of Virginia, pp. 15, 50, 54, 69, 74, 82, 86, 90, 91, 116 (top); Illinois State Historical Library, pp. 16, 30; The Maitland Art Center, p. 17; Library of Congress, pp. 20, 25, 26, 28, 32, 33, 34, 39, 40, 42, 43, 46, 51, 60, 64, 67, 71, 73, 78, 88, 92, 95, 99, 100, 101, 106, 109, 110, 120, 121, 128, 130, 131, 132, 133; Metropolitan Museum of Art, Gift of Mr. and Mrs. Carl Stoeckel, 1897, p. 21 (left); Metropolitan Museum of Art, Arthur H. Hearn Fund, 1950, p. 21 (right); University of Michigan Museum of Art, Bequest of Henry C. Lewis, 1895.80, p. 23; Minneapolis Public Library and Information Center, pp. 37, 113, 118; Abraham Lincoln Museum, Lincoln Memorial University, pp. 42, 87; White House Historical Society, pp. 48, 52; Lincoln Museum, Ft. Wayne, Indiana, p. 56; Collections of the Lehigh County Historical Society, p. 63; U.S. Naval Academy Museum, pp. 76, 81; National Portrait Gallery, London, p. 80; Architect of the Capitol, painting held by United States Senate Art Gallery, p. 84; Dictionary of American Portraits, p. 66; The Newark Museum, gift of Mrs. Hannah Corbin Carter, Horace K. Corbin Jr., Robert S. Corbin, William D. Corbin, and Mrs. Clementine Corbin Day in memory of their parents, Hannah Stockton Corbin and Horace Kellogg Corbin 1966, p. 97; Surratt House Museum, p. 102; National Portrait Gallery, Smithsonian Institution, p. 104; Bettmann, p. 112; Appomattox National Historical Park, p. 114; Argossy Bookstore, New York, pp. 122, 123; West Point Museum, United States Military Academy, New York, p. 124; National Portrait Gallery, Washington, D.C. / Art Resource, back cover.